DECODING GLOBAL GROWTH

DECODING GLOBAL GROWTH

How successful companies scale internationally

TRENA BLAIR

Trena Blair has been on the frontier of business trends for decades – building relationships and operating globally. She brings this experience and the associated perspective to a wonderfully insightful look at what it takes to succeed and grow across international markets. Outlining the evolution in leadership, governance, business process and pitching for funding that accompanies and enables successful scaling, the book brings together wisdom from business leaders in multiple markets to highlight the nexus between risk management and governance as enablers of global growth. It is likely to become the 'go-to' handbook for entrepreneurs keen to move beyond home markets.

Leslie Martin, non-executive director and advisor

Trena is extremely professional, personable and always willing to help another person or company progress up the ladder or achieve success. Trena knows the US market exceptionally well, her connections are exemplary, and she is an excellent 'Sherpa guide' to anybody looking to enter and summit this market. Her book is a must-read for anyone looking to launch quickly and effectively in the United States. She is also a very generous person with her knowledge and time, and we are fortunate to call her a friend.

Phillip Campbell, cognitive scientist, *USA Today* and *Wall Street Journal* bestselling author, *Brain Habits: The Science of Subconscious Success*

Trena Blair provides a detailed blueprint for leaders looking to expand their businesses globally. Her use of relevant case studies showcases her expertise in launching Australian companies into the United States, providing important lessons that are applicable to all of us.

April Palmerlee, Chief Executive Officer, American Chamber of Commerce in Australia

Trena Blair takes her own experiences of growing her company FD Global Connections and builds what is a useful and practical handbook for global business development. She taps the experiences of entrepreneurs and founders – from industries as varied as digital marketing, financial services, transportation and medical appliances – who have made that leap, and shares them as insights that others can consider, follow or adapt to their own needs. The result is a rare look into how real companies have been successful, or pivoted, as they plan their overseas growth. Insights into five overseas markets go past the obvious national stereotypes to highlight the subtle nuances that make a difference: one size does not fit all. Have this book near at hand when planning how to make the first steps to becoming a global business.

Alan Smith, Head of Strategic Business Communications, Digivizer

I met Trena in NYC just as she started FD Global Connections, and the phenomenal success she's achieved in growing her own business globally is the best testimony of the capability she offers to clients, many of whom I've met as they joined and then successfully scaled their businesses into the US market. And now, this generous catalyst is offering her precious experience to every ambitious entrepreneur. Even if you're still early in your business lifecycle, these frameworks will be valuable in laying the right foundations upon which to build your global expansion strategy.

Who doesn't love a good basic recipe that you can twist and scale with reliability, predictability and probable success?

Annalie Killian, global soul and Catalyst for Magic

To Mum and Dad, for instilling in me from an early age that anything is possible, and whose boundless love will forever sustain me.

And to my husband, Christian, for your enduring love and profound inspiration to live an authentic life.

First published in 2024 by FD Global Connections Pty Ltd

© Trena Blair 2024
The moral rights of the author have been asserted.

All rights reserved. Except as permitted under the *Australian Copyright Act 1968* (for example, a fair dealing for the purposes of study, research, criticism or review), no part of this book may be reproduced, stored in a retrieval system, communicated or transmitted in any form or by any means without prior written permission.

All inquiries should be made to the author.

A catalogue entry for this book is available from the National Library of Australia.

ISBN: 978-1-923007-30-7

Printed in Australia by Pegasus
Book production and text design by Publish Central
Cover design by Pipeline Design

The paper this book is printed on is environmentally friendly.

Disclaimer: The material in this publication is of the nature of general comment only, and does not represent professional advice. It is not intended to provide specific guidance for particular circumstances and it should not be relied on as the basis for any decision to take action or not take action on any matter which it covers. Readers should obtain professional advice where appropriate, before making any such decision. To the maximum extent permitted by law, the author and associated entities and publisher disclaim all responsibility and liability to any person, arising directly or indirectly from any person taking or not taking action based on the information in this publication.

CONTENTS

FOREWORD

With *Decoding Global Growth*, Trena Blair contributes an invaluable compendium of knowledge and advice for founders looking for tools to expand their companies beyond their own borders. Trena is way too smart to promise this is a one-size-fits-all solution, but this book does offer an invaluable framework for this complex and potentially perilous endeavour.

Trena frames how to think about growing a company to have a global presence based on three concepts:

- *The Business Growth Lifecycle*, which identifies the roadmap typical of companies as they grow and mature.
- *The Process Scalability Formula*, which outlines how your business's readiness to scale is based on Repeatability + Predictability + Probability.
- *The Global Scalability Audit*, which allows you to test your business's potential for scalability across five key areas.

Using historical references, case studies and interviews with CEOs who have successfully expanded their own companies globally, you will find examples of companies that have achieved global growth when starting from Australia, the US, the UK, Singapore and Japan.

Trena Blair's goal is for you to be successful. (And hopefully, happy.)

Charles Dickens, in his novel *David Copperfield*, wrote this pertinent statement:

Annual income twenty pounds, annual expenditure nineteen nineteen and six, result happiness. Annual income twenty pounds, annual expenditure twenty pounds ought and six, result misery.

Read this book. Reference this book. Be sure you have a copy in your business library for the day, should you be so lucky, that you begin to think about taking your company global.

Marcos Dinnerstein
Founder, *A Better Mousetrap* newsletter,
former editor of Digital.nyc

INTRODUCTION

In 2007, I transferred to New York when my husband accepted a promising appointment in the healthcare industry. I left behind a network of friends and colleagues who were important social supports, and I felt quite alone. Yet, it was an exciting time for us both as we embarked on a new life in one of the world's most famous cities.

The creative energy that New York offers is palpable at street level. New Yorkers are renowned for their boundless enthusiasm and can-do attitude to almost anything, including business endeavours. Self-doubt and timidity are not part of the lexicon in the Big Apple. I decided to incorporate some of these elements and use them to inspire a new phase in my life. In so doing, I stepped out of my comfort zone, broadened my cultural horizons and expanded my business opportunities. My first interaction was, in fact, with the doorman in my apartment building. And I soon discovered that New Yorkers are open-minded, inquisitive, engaging and always ready to discuss a business deal.

As I settled into New York life, I quickly adopted a 'New York state of mind', learning to drink filter coffee and embracing the joys of winter afternoons strolling through Central Park. Quickly enough, I built a broad network of personal acquaintances featuring prominent commercial and business stakeholders throughout the city. I realised more than ever the importance of fostering close personal and business relationships to build a trusted network.

I believe it is incumbent on all of us to never take the goodwill and collaboration of others for granted and, secondly, to share learnings with others. This has been my philosophy in business and is the fundamental reason I have written this book. I hope that paying it forward in this way benefits readers interested in transitioning their business into a global marketplace.

About this book

So, what does this have to do with this *Decoding Global Growth*?

Global expansion is fundamentally about cultivating local connections in the target market. By the time I founded FD Global Connections in 2014, my network in New York City and across the United States was extensive, and my focus turned to connecting clients to this network.

However, while a strong network is critical, leaders require further support as their business expands into foreign markets to achieve their growth objectives. In this book, I introduce three new concepts I have designed to support leaders. The first is the Business Growth Lifecycle, which identifies the roadmap typical of companies as they grow and mature. Based on my experience and insights from discussions with global CEOs, I identify four foundational elements – leadership, governance, funding (pitching) and process management – and how they evolve through the business cycle. This feeds into my second new concept: the Process Scalability Formula. This formula outlines how your business's readiness to scale is based on Repeatability + Predictability + Probability. In this book, I share how you can use these three factors to deeply analyse your processes as you prepare to expand into new markets – and help you answer that big question, 'What does a scalable business look like?' I provide further help to answer this question with my third new concept: the Global Scalability Audit. I designed this audit so you can test your business's potential for scalability across five key areas.

As a business owner, I also understand the challenges in identifying your target client in a new, foreign market. In the following chapters, I share how I have created my business's global pathway using a detailed go-to-market approach and the deep research it calls for.

With these insights, at FD Global Connections, we design and build brand awareness for clients that resonates with their target market.

The ultimate success of global growth is generating revenue and profitability. Determining your profitability and determining your distribution model are core. Many factors require assessment to ensure you have a solid team representing your business. International border closures during the COVID-19 pandemic have resulted in new distribution models that continue to be leveraged by savvy business leaders, and these will shape global expansion strategies for many years to come.

However, not all businesses are ready to expand into a foreign market. The vision may exist, but global ventures often need rigorous research and financial and strategic preparedness.

Along with the expertise gained through my own experience, I also included through the book interviews with CEOs, who reveal deep insights into their companies, including critical strategies they have adopted for success. Also, I spotlight five key global growth markets – Australia, the United States, the United Kingdom, Singapore and Japan – and chart the expansion and market-entry journeys.

Researching this book has taken me to an extraordinary range of places, from boardrooms to the histories of global trade. (Who would have thought that Pharaohs, Venetian merchants and a renowned global explorer would feature in such a book?) It has taken me from Sydney to New York and back many times over. (I have the air miles to prove it!) Importantly, it has expanded my own horizons in ways that looking outward at the world with endless curiosity can only do.

I hope you enjoy reading this book as much as I enjoyed bringing it to life.

How to use this book

My experience is in working with clients expanding their business into the United States; however, this book can be used by leaders with international growth ambitions into any market. This book, therefore, is for leaders who seek an understanding of the necessary steps to expand into a foreign market. You can either read as a whole, or cherry-pick specific chapters or parts, depending on where your business is on its global growth pathway.

I have divided the book into four parts:

- *Part I: Setting the globalisation scene* contains three chapters, opening with a figure from history whom you may not have heard of – Queen Hatshepsut (the forgotten Pharaoh), who was reportedly the first female in international trade. I weave in historical elements with modern-day case studies and capture insights from my experience and discussions with other CEOs. In this part, I also introduce the Business Global Lifecycle and the four foundational elements of leadership, governance, funding and process management.

- *Part II: Laying the foundations for global growth* dedicates a chapter to each of the four foundational elements. A scaleup's core objective is to achieve sustainable growth. This requires deep consideration to ensure the structure, controls and metrics are established and regularly monitored. My Process Scalability Formula and Global Scalability Audit (covered in chapter 7) provide new approaches to identifying, analysing and measuring core processes for growth businesses.

- *Part III: Focusing on the key pillars for global growth* discusses three critical areas of your business that must be closely managed as you scale. These are customers, distribution models and building your global brand. The strategies outlined in this part are designed to highlight learnings from where other businesses have failed and spotlight the value of the smart allocation of precious time and resources throughout the global expansion process.

- *Part IV: The top five global markets* captures interviews with experts in key markets for global growth, including Australia, the United States, the United Kingdom, Singapore and Japan. This section offers actionable insights from experts who live and work in each market and insights into their knowledge of history, culture, leadership and lessons for leaders considering those markets.

At the end of each chapter in parts I to III, I also include a dedicated page outlining the key takeaways and a prompt question for you to consider and respond to.

One model does not fit every business

Every business is unique and must forge its journey that reflects its vision, company values, capability and capacity. This book does not claim to offer a methodology for all businesses and does not guarantee international success. But it does contain the knowledge I have amassed throughout my international career, and what I have observed and applied to my business and clients over the past 10 years.

I have written this book for business leaders with ambitions to develop a global growth strategy. It is for those who seek insights from others who have successfully forged their way into the international arena. In writing this book, I fervently hope that the information presented assists you in preparing to embark on one of the most exciting journeys a business leader can undertake – to expand your business's global reach and influence and help offer solutions to your customers' problems.

However, my overall aim in writing this book is to save you the most precious commodity for all business owners – time. I wish you the best of luck as you get started.

PART I

SETTING THE GLOBALISATION SCENE

Welcome to part I of *Decoding Global Growth*, where we embark on a fascinating journey through time and delve into the intricacies of global trade. This section, comprising three chapters, lays the foundation for understanding the complex tapestry of globalisation.

In chapter 1, we commence our exploration with an intriguing historical figure who, until relatively recently, was overlooked – Queen Hatshepsut, the 'forgotten' Pharaoh. Although her name may not be familiar, Queen Hatshepsut played a pivotal role in international trade, making her mark as the purported first female leader to engage in commerce beyond the borders of her kingdom. In this chapter, I explore the relationship between the multifaceted impacts of globalisation and nationalisation, while outlining how its trajectory can be influenced by various factors such as political ideologies, economic conditions, technological advances and global events.

As we journey onward, chapter 2 draws upon a rich tapestry of historical elements, as I also weave in contemporary case studies to illustrate the ever-evolving landscape of global business. These stories, infused with insights from my own experiences and thought-provoking discussions with fellow CEOs, bring to life the triumphs, challenges and lessons of real-world global trade.

Chapter 3 introduces a ground-breaking concept – the Business Growth Lifecycle. I developed this framework to serve as a compass, guiding you through the five stages and dynamics of a business – from startup, to growth and maturity – and all through the lens of global expansion. I explore the distinct stages of growth for a business, from humble origins to a global presence, shedding light on the four foundational elements essential for thriving in the global arena: leadership, governance, funding (pitching) and process management.

By immersing yourself in this comprehensive model, you can gain a profound understanding of the factors influencing success in the global marketplace.

With the foundational concepts outlined in part I as our guide, we embark on a transformative voyage through the intricate web of global trade. By illuminating the stories of forgotten trailblazers, incorporating contemporary case studies, and providing invaluable insights from seasoned CEOs, I hope to equip you with the knowledge and wisdom necessary to navigate the challenges and opportunities of the global marketplace. Together, we will decode the secrets of global growth and unlock the pathway to your unparalleled success.

CHAPTER 1

BLENDING THE PAST WITH THE PRESENT

She knew her journey would be difficult, but she had little choice. Essential products for her people were becoming scarce, traditional trading partners had become expensive and supply unreliable. She identified a new source of exotic goods, but it was in the distant Land of Punt, not traded with for many centuries. So, she built five ships, each 70 feet long, and, with only 210 sailors and soldiers, she sailed rivers and uncharactered canals to secure valuable products. She returned home after 25 days with incense for temples, frankincense and myrrh trees, amber, gold, lapis-lazuli, ivory, precious woods and wild animals. Her courageous pioneering spirit resulted in success, and she became one of history's earliest women to have an important profile in international trade.

The name of this remarkable woman is Queen Hatshepsut. Her name means 'She is First Among Noble Women' – and she was a

Statue of Queen Hatshepsut, Dutch National Museum of Antiquities[1]

powerful Pharaoh, reigning as Queen of Egypt, and the fifth ruler of the 18th Dynasty, from 1473 to 1458 BCE. Previously overshadowed by that other female Pharaoh (Cleopatra, who ruled Egypt between 51 and 30 BCE), Hatshepsut is now more broadly recognised for her achievements in sculpture and the decorative arts and in building temples and monuments – including her mortuary temple at Deir el-Bahri. However, beyond these achievements was her focus on renewing international trade with not only the Land of Punt, but also Western Asia and the Aegean islands, resulting in a period of economic prosperity for Egypt.

Human beings have always been curious creatures. We have travelled from one place to another throughout history, encountering different tribes, cultures and nations. Our need to explore faraway places to seek new experiences, share knowledge and solve problems, similar to Hatshepsut and her pioneering journeys, made globalisation inevitable.

Globalisation is more formally defined by the Peterson Institute for International Economics as 'the growing interdependence of the world's cultures, economies and populations, brought about by the movement and exchange of goods, people, services, capital, technologies and cultural practices across international borders.'[2] Globalisation is a term that describes much of what makes the world feel connected. We each see it in activities such as ease of overseas travel and access to foreign products and services simply via a search on the internet.

A key driver of globalisation is how communication has improved and evolved. Looking back to the Middle Ages, we find handwritten news sheets developed in Venice, Italy. Authors anonymously wrote these to communicate political, military and economic opinions, using a complex web of couriers for distribution. Germany was also soon producing handwritten newsletters, and it was here, in around 1436, that Johannes Gutenberg invented the printing press (although the printing process was not yet automated). The print press revolutionised communication and led to printing modernisation toward the end of the 17th century.

Moving forward to the 19th century, the introduction of steam power enabled ship propulsion, resulting in faster, more reliable and heavier loads, thereby transforming the transportation of goods around the globe. Meanwhile, the introduction of radio, electric telegraph and telephone continued transforming communications.

To my mind, the most notable impact of technological advancement has been the dramatic increase in our ability to exchange ideas, engage and connect. The computer and the internet have made it easier to bring people closer together than ever before. Messages are sent with a simple tap on the screen of a phone, and a video call can instantly bring us closer regardless of where we are in the world. Indeed, the rapid advancement in technology over the last few decades has led to the proliferation of transportation and communication options, which, in turn, has sped up globalisation.

Globalisation, 'Globalisation 2.0' or nationalism?

Globalisation is an enduring theme that has evolved throughout the centuries in response to innovation, technological advances and government collaborations. It has resulted in the interconnectedness and interdependence of countries, economies and cultures, and given rise to greater opportunities for businesses to access foreign markets. Governments around the globe are removing trade barriers and introducing free trade policies to increase economic and financial prosperity. According to the World Trade Organization (WTO), the world's imports and exports have significantly increased in the last three decades. In growth economies, the increased exchange of knowledge and technology, and increased rates of international cooperation boosted the share of global exports from 34 per cent to 47 per cent and the share of imports from 29 per cent to 42 per cent between 1980 and 2011.[3]

According to latest research from Statista, "In 2022, the global trade value of goods exported throughout the world amounted to approximately 24.9 trillion U.S. dollars at current prices. In comparison, this figure stood at around 6.45 trillion U.S. dollars in 2000."[4]

Olaf Groth is a well-known scholar and expert in the field of technology, innovation and global business. He has written extensively on the topic of 'Globalisation 2.0'.[5] Globalisation 2.0, as described by Olaf Groth, refers to the current phase of globalisation driven by emerging technologies, such as artificial intelligence, robotics and the Internet of Things (IoT). It represents a shift from the traditional model of globalisation, which primarily focused on the global movement of goods, services and capital. Globalisation 2.0 is characterised by the digital transformation of industries, the rise of interconnectedness, and the increasing integration of emerging markets into the global economy.

One of the key aspects of Globalisation 2.0 is the exponential growth of data and the ability to collect, analyse and leverage data for business purposes. This data-driven approach enables companies to gain insights into consumer or business behaviour, market trends and competitive dynamics, allowing them to make more informed decisions and develop innovative products and services.

Understanding Globalisation 2.0 is crucial for business leaders for several reasons:

1. *Market opportunities:* Globalisation 2.0 opens up markets and customer segments that were previously inaccessible. By understanding the dynamics of this new phase, business leaders can identify growth opportunities and expand their operations to emerging markets.

2. *Competitive advantage:* Embracing Globalisation 2.0 can provide a competitive edge. Companies that effectively leverage emerging technologies such as artificial intelligence (AI) or additive printing can streamline their operations, enhance productivity and develop innovative business models, giving them an advantage over traditional competitors.

3. *Disruption and adaptation:* Globalisation 2.0 brings disruptive changes to industries and business environments. Business

leaders need to understand these changes to anticipate and adapt to them effectively. Failure to do so can result in obsolescence and loss of market share.

4. *Talent and workforce development:* Globalisation 2.0 requires a skilled and adaptable workforce. Business leaders need to understand the changing nature of work and the skills needed to thrive in a digital economy. They must invest in talent development and create a culture of continuous learning to stay ahead.

5. *Ethical and social implications:* Globalisation 2.0 raises ethical and social issues, such as data privacy, cybersecurity and the impact of automation on employment. Business leaders must be aware of these concerns and navigate them responsibly to build trust with customers, employees and stakeholders.

Globalisation 2.0 represents a new phase of globalisation driven by emerging technologies. Understanding its dynamics is essential for business leaders to identify opportunities, stay competitive, adapt to disruptions, develop a skilled workforce, and address ethical and social challenges. By embracing Globalisation 2.0, companies can position themselves for success in the evolving global business landscape.

However, recent events such as COVID-19 and Brexit also point to a shift away from globalisation, and a situation where politicians have called for domestic champions to rise, rather than continue to converge with other countries for trade purposes.

The *New York Times'* opinion editor, David Brooks, captured this sentiment best in his article 'Globalization is over. The global culture wars have begun'.[6] He said:

In country after country, highly nationalistic movements have arisen to insist on national sovereignty and to restore national pride: Modi in India, Recep Tayyip Erdoğan in Turkey, Trump in the United States, Boris Johnson in Britain. To hell with cosmopolitanism and global convergence, they say.

We're going to make our own country great again in our own way. Many globalists completely underestimated the power of nationalism to drive history.

Counter this opinion with research from McKinsey Global stating that no region is close to being self-sufficient and, during the course of the last five years, the largest economies have not systematically diversified the origin of imports.[7]

The choice between globalisation and nationalism for business leaders doesn't have to be so stark; they can exist in tandem. These forces also offer clues as to how businesses can begin to think about expansion – for example, bringing new ideas, products and services into another market can be valuable to their economy. However, businesses must also adapt to each local market to be a successful international enterprise.

Against this background of globalisation and nationalisation, expanding into new global markets continues to be a viable and highly attractive proposition for many business leaders. Expanding internationally opens access to lucrative new markets and a massive pool of potential clients. For example, the population of Australia only represents 0.33 per cent of the global population. Looking beyond the immediate horizon opens businesses up to a greater world of opportunity to scale and grow their reach and influence.

Beginning the business expansion journey

When does a business know it's ready to expand globally? Tech Nation defines a 'scaleup' – or a business potentially ready to expand – as a company that has maintained a 20 per cent growth rate yearly for at least three years with a minimum of 10 employees.[8] While this is an important guideline, in my 10 years of experience working with clients to expand internationally, other important factors should be taken into consideration. The first being whether or not the business is ready to expand into a foreign market. To determine this, I ask the following questions:

- Can you articulate the strategic objective for expanding globally?
- Does the leadership team have an established network in the target market?
- Does your business have the capital for global expansion?
- Does the business have robust systems and measurable processes to support a significant increase in volume?
- Does the business have the leadership experience, discipline and capacity to expand globally?
- Do staff have the experience, capability and resilience to support an international market in addition to the current home market?
- Is there interest from potential customers or future partners?

These are just some of the critical topics I cover in much more detail through this book, providing ways you as a business leader can address these issues as you consider global expansion.

Learning from others

Many businesses have enjoyed significant local success but failed to make the overseas leap. For savvy business leaders, building a business platform to support global expansion, undertaking market research and adapting to customer needs is imperative when beginning to operate overseas:

1. *Global expansion is a process that should not be rushed.* This process should be undertaken with careful planning and a realistic understanding of the current health of the business and its potential. A leader's first task in building a global business is determining if their business has the capability and capacity to expand internationally. If these are not first understood, your efforts will likely waste time, effort and precious funds.

2. *Leaders must shift their mindset.* Leaders must learn to assess and monitor business processes to achieve scalability, and specifically consider whether core processes of sales, customer support

and marketing can be repeated in new markets to achieve a consistent outcome.

Your focus needs to be honed on:

- designing and supporting a business structure based on functional hierachies
- implementing automation of front- and back-office processes
- ensuring that data and measurement systems are established to track outputs
- cultivating an organisational culture that is fit for purpose.

3. *Leaders often forget the startup reality.* When a business is launched into a new market, it becomes a startup again. Leaders need to focus again on product-market fit and customer validation in the new market. Offering a solution to a problem that truly exists in the new market of entry is important – as is noting that the problem may not present as identical from market to market.

4. *Leaders often show a lack of cultural awareness and understanding of the nuances of the market.* Leaders must understand the local customs and protocols that guide how business is done in a particular market. You must adapt how you approach aspects such as networking, sales pitching and your use of local language nuances in order to succeed.

5. *Business models often focus on gaining profitability from product sales.* Many leaders believe that a business will keep growing if customers keep purchasing their product. However, customers rarely want to repurchase the same product. They want new features, greater usability and added value. Retaining clients with additional product features requires investment, which small profit margins cannot cover. So, unless your business has secured investment or has adopted a diverse revenue strategy before expanding, it will ultimately fail.

6. *Leaders expect their local support team to manage unrealistic time zone differences.* I have observed various staffing models

to support new markets – ranging from local support teams trying to manage offshore clients in reverse time zones, to catapulting existing experienced leaders into the offshore market. Others have preferred to recruit a local leader with an existing network and lived cultural knowledge to develop the business. An effective hiring strategy that includes representation offshore to provide local market intelligence is essential for your business to thrive.

7. *Building the local brand requires time and investment.* As I have mentioned, business leaders often forget they are a startup again and that a significant budget is required to build a brand in the new market. A common challenge for marketing teams is ensuring the business looks like a local business – or at least has been integrated into the local business landscape through a localised marketing strategy. This matters – a US consumer, for example, prefers to buy from a US business. Therefore, it's imperative to develop a brand strategy that dovetails into your marketing activity. Providing a website with pricing, images, logos and services that reflect the market you are moving into is just the start of building your brand.

8. *Governance and risk management frameworks can fail.* World events can have an immediate and detrimental impact on supply chains, causing significant disruption. The manufacturing and agricultural sectors felt this during COVID-19, and these sectors are only starting to recover at the time of writing. Therefore, ensuring that you've completed appropriate risk assessments and established disaster recovery plans is essential.

Are you ready?

It's fair to say that for many leaders, expanding globally is a tangible and necessary step to access new clients. However, to be successful, significant preparation and planning, backed by detailed evaluation and analysis, is vital to minimise the risks. What's also required to succeed is the ability to make intelligent, realistic – and often diffi-cult – strategic choices.

While no two businesses are the same, what you will discover in the following chapters from the interviews with CEOs and the insights from my own experience is that companies that successfully expand internationally have common attributes. These include the following:

- building a network of international contacts
- the ability to tell a great story about the problem they are solving
- scalability and repeatability of critical processes within the business
- laser-sharp research on the country targeted for global expansion
- international leadership experience
- governance oversight with strong risk management.

I discuss these attributes and how to build them throughout this book.

***

Earlier I introduced Queen Hatshepsut as an example of a powerful woman who reached beyond her immediate horizon to achieve eco-nomic gains for her kingdom and people. Of course, she would not recognise the world today, but she would see common themes in the current globalisation perspective and the geopolitical considerations of her world. However, notwithstanding our reliance on technology, there has been one constant, primary objective throughout history when it comes to international trade: to secure products and services that improve overall living standards. Queen Hatshepsut was extra-ordinary and taught governments and business owners an important lesson – to monitor trends, identify opportunities and have the courage to develop strategies to secure their future with new partners, wherever they may be around the globe.

Top 5 insights from this chapter

1. Globalisation has evolved throughout the centuries in response to innovation, technological advances and government collaborations. It brought benefits such as increased trade, technological advancement and money movement across borders.

2. The choice between 'Globalisation 2.0' and nationalism for business leaders doesn't have to be so stark; these two forces do exist in tandem.

3. Tech Nation defines a 'scaleup' – or a business ready to expand – as a company that has maintained a 20 per cent growth rate yearly for at least three years with a minimum of 10 employees. This is a useful guide; however, every business is unique and will establish their individual parameters for global expansion.

4. The journey can be tumultuous for businesses expanding globally, with approximately 70 per cent failing.

5. For savvy business leaders, building the platform to grow globally from the start, evolving with market shifts and adapting to customer needs is imperative when planning to operate overseas.

Self-reflection: Queen Hatshepsut was the first female Pharaoh of Egypt. She was a powerful woman in international trade who serves as a touchstone for our ambition to reach beyond local markets, and leaves a remarkable legacy. What is the legacy you wish to leave with your business?

_____

_____

_____

_____

_____

_____

_____

_____

_____

_____

_____

CHAPTER 2

PIONEERING ENTREPRENEURS FROM THE PAST

Without stones, there is no arch.

Marco Polo, Venetian entrepreneur, in the Italo Calvino novel *Invisible Cities*

I was seated at a bar in Venice, Italy, enjoying the obligatory afternoon spritz, when I noticed a curious sign displaying the word 'Bancogiro'. The geographic reality of Venice means it is one of the best-preserved cities in the world, so I realised the name most likely reflected an interesting story. I started researching 'Bancogiro', and what I uncovered was fascinating from a globalisation perspective.

The first national European bank, the Banco di Rialto, was established in Venice in 1587.[1] It was replaced in 1619 by Bancogiro, a public bank positioned opposite the church of San Giacomo di Rialto, known today as 'San Giacometto', at the foot of the famous Rialto Bridge. These institutions were the predecessors of the Bank of England and the First Bank of the United States. However, the deeper I went with my research, the more intrigued I became by the similarities between the present-day complex global commercial trade and its more humble beginnings, which took root almost 1000 years ago.

Notably, the site of Bancogiro was close to the Grand Canal, used for transporting international imports, and where merchants strategically located their warehouses. These early merchants of Venice were innovators who operated in an era when few formal regulations existed to support money exchange for goods. Little did the merchants realise it at the time, but what they were on their way to establishing – with the invention of payment mechanisms to secure international trade – was the foundation of globalisation as we know it today.

Innovation in financial transfer had flourished in the region since the earliest known foreign exchange contract in Genoa in 1156, when two brothers borrowed 115 Genoese pounds and agreed to reimburse the bank's agents in Constantinople with the sum of 460 bezants one month after they arrived in that city.[2] The forward-looking leaders in Genoa established the Banco di San Giorgio in 1407. They are credited with 10 significant financial innovations, including establishing a creditors association, letters of exchange and a clearing house. Today, the rules applied to these instruments and international settlements remain.

Genoa and Venice were economic and geopolitical rivals in the Middle Ages. Of course, they shared some common elements: the importance of trade and the undermining of profit by unscrupulous merchants who did not pay taxes and custom dues. So, it was up to the merchants from both powerful cities to work out how to trade their goods – domestically and internationally – to ensure fair and timely payment.

With remarkable ingenuity in the absence of formal financial instruments to secure the transfer of money, the powerful Venetian merchants worked with the Senate to pass approximately 40 Acts, enabling, among other things, the first debt-payment instrument – known today as the IOU. In so

'Bancogiro' and eponymous bar at the Rialto, Venice 2019[3]

doing, they initiated the first recorded use of double-entry bookkeeping.[4]

The payment solutions created and implemented by the Venetian and Genoese merchants were ideated and funded by merchants using personal wealth. They created new products and processes that improved security and trust among a complex network of interests previously marked by distrust and secrecy.

It's an understatement to say that these new payment mechanisms changed the world of trade. Whereas once a transaction was typically made with a handshake, it was now done with a simple yet effective legal document. Merchants found not paying their taxes or custom dues were forced out of the industry, which no longer tolerated them.

The developments of the Venetians and Genovese were the foundations of today's financial services products and solutions. But they also, probably unknowingly, created something else – they set formal ground rules, or 'principles' of operating on an international scale.

Characteristics of successful global companies

Globalisation has opened doors for businesses wanting to expand internationally; however, taking a business to new heights is not necessarily easy. So, it's worth taking note of the following characteristics of successful global companies.[5]

Understanding different cultures

Companies need to conduct in-depth research on the local practices, values and cultural nuances of the target country. These must be understood before decisions are made about organisational structures and policies relating to working hours, allowances for religious rituals, and other local expectations and requirements.

At the beginning of this chapter, I introduced you to Venice, a city that celebrated its merchants and explorers for returning with treasures from faraway lands. Marco Polo is one of its most famous sons – returning with salt, pepper, spices and jewels from the Orient.

Living from 1254 to 1342 and travelling around Asia Minor for 25 years, Polo was the exemplar of a Venetian entrepreneur. His inspirational life story has become legend, and is still well known today. As a foreigner travelling in a vast, unknown land, Polo spent considerable time in China – first and foremost, observing the people and learning about their customs, language, food and social structures. In fact, while trade and business were important, these were secondary considerations. This is because Polo and his family, along with other Venetian and Genovese entrepreneurs, understood the importance of building relationships as a foundation to business success.

Polo's story comes down to us because of the fantastical stories he told after returning to Venice after 25 years in the Orient at the court of Kublai Khan. His entrepreneurial feats were above and beyond the norms of the day, and seem the equivalent today of looking for silks and spices on the dark side of the moon. Some sources argue that Polo was the first to make significant, tangible connections between Eastern and Western cultures. He astonished his compatriots with descriptions of places that Europeans had never explored. On his death, he famously stated, 'I have not told the half of what I saw'.

Marco Polo also brings us to an important element that applies to all business leaders: curiosity or, in modern-day terminology, a growth mindset. New experiences and opportunities across cultures, languages, religions and local customs through exchanging knowledge and information are vital for business leaders to expand into new markets successfully.

International experience

Studies have shown that companies that do well internationally usually have a founder or C-Suite leader on their team who is a first-generation immigrant from a foreign country.[6] This makes sense because international experience makes it easier for companies to understand how to optimise their operations to cater to the needs of local market audiences. They do not fear exploring a new market because they have direct knowledge and experience of these kinds of explorations – or, at the very least, a global awareness of how people live and work worldwide.

According to the National Venture Capital Association (NVCA), more than 25 per cent of all startups founded in San Francisco from 1997 to 2012 were founded by immigrants.[7] In addition, first-generation American or foreign-born immigrants have established more than 43 per cent of all Fortune 500 companies.[8] Examples include Google's co-founder Sergey Brin (Russia) and Facebook's co-founder Eduardo Saverin (Brazil). Many major companies are also led by immigrants, such as Microsoft's CEO Satya Nadella (India).

In Australia, according to the CGU Insurance *Migrant Small Business Report*, 33 per cent of all small businesses are founded by migrants.[9]

In my experience, clients with executives with lived experience in the target country, either as an immigrant or as an expatriate, have a deeper appreciation of the challenges of building a global business than those companies with employees with no international experience.

International business partners

Most successful businesses have a strong network of trusted advisors – sometimes known as key opinion leaders or ambassadors – who have helped them expand internationally. Finding the right partner to smooth your expansion into a market is highly beneficial. These partners can offer unique, highly localised qualitative insights, and product and competitive intelligence that cannot be gained from reading reports and statistics alone.

Establishing a partnership program requires a unique strategy that should encapsulate the following:

- profiling your ideal partner, starting with alignment of your strategic direction and company values
- researching and undertaking the interviewing process
- developing an outline of your compensation structure
- establishing the onboarding process

- determining the rules of engagement, including measures of success.

I discuss distribution strategies and sales partnerships in much more detail in chapter 9.

Inclusive work environment

A common trait of successful global businesses is an inclusive work environment. Research has shown that employees who work in an inclusive environment are more engaged and have a higher retention rate.[10] Industry analyst John Bersin said it best when he stated that an inclusive work environment 'lets people speak up, innovate, share new ideas, and help others without risk'. Companies can cultivate this sentiment by considering the following when building company culture:

- defining a purpose that each employee resonates with
- developing a global strategy to find, develop and retain talent
- identifying and incorporating target market culture and employee benefits (for example, medical, retirement) into your talent strategy
- defining clear roles, responsibilities and delegation of duties
- monitoring leaders' adherence to company values in every decision
- implementing a measurement system to track employee engagement, resilience and motivation.

Measuring success

Identifying core processes and establishing robust systems to measure and report them is essential. It's also important to communicate results throughout the organisation regularly. This matters for several reasons, not least because the sooner companies identify a failure point, the sooner they can engage their teams, pivot and the more likely they are to succeed.

In chapter 7, I outline my Process Scalability Formula, which focuses on how you can use three essential elements to measure success as your business progresses through the various phases of global expansion.

With these insights into characteristics, how do companies pursuing global growth integrate these elements? I sat down to discuss this with Skander Malcolm, CEO and Managing Director of OFX since 2017.

OFX: A MODERN-DAY CASE STUDY

I introduced you to the financial product revolutions from Venice and Genoa at the beginning of this chapter. In this case study, I am drawing your attention to an Australian financial institution with a significant global presence that, like many other companies in the financial services industry, leveraged those historical payment methods and created modern-day versions of products and services to build international success.

Matthew Gilmour worked full-time in the financial services industry while running a side hustle. Working in his garage, Gilmour built an information-only website to assist small business importers in processing their payments. In 1998, Gilmour established the company as OzForex to build a better and fairer way to move money worldwide. By 2005, in an interview with *The Age*, he says it had got 'out of control'.[11]

Today, OFX (as OzForex is now known) is an online foreign exchange and payment company providing money transfer services to clients including MoneyGram, Travelex, Capital One 360 and Macquarie International Money Transfers. According to OFX's Annual Report 2023, OFX transferred AUD $39 billion for clients worldwide.

OFX's vision is to become the 'world's leading cross-border payments specialist', and the company employs over 715 staff in 12 offices around the globe. OFX company values are:

- Always keep learning; share your expertise, learn from others.
- Get the right stuff done; own it, execute it, deliver the exceptional.

- Inspire client confidence; keep the client at the centre of everything we do.
- Push boundaries; discover what is possible.
- We're better together; we are stronger as one team.

During my discussion with Skander, he shared four foundational pillars critical to his company's global success.

Listen to the customer

To fully understand OFX's client needs, extensive local market research uncovered the following essential client requirements: faster, affordable and frictionless payment transfer experiences.

Skander explained that each market leader is responsible for OFX's distinctive customer value proposition – to deliver a competitively priced and trusted client experience by combining digital and human support and expertise.

These product insights and strategic global footprint of the markets they operate in give OFX a clear competitive advantage. This focus and concentration of effort enables Skander and his team to develop deep, profitable client relationships.

However, I learned from Skander that while understanding his clients' requirements was essential, another critical issue that OFX needed to overcome was building trust.

Build trust

As OFX's global footprint expanded, Skander's main obstacle to gaining market share was building trust in an online payments platform at a time when clients preferred to conduct their financial transactions at physical banks. OFX needed to design and build its client-facing systems and underlying processes, which clients could easily navigate and trust their payment instructions would be followed. Their processes were deliberately designed to create certainty for customers about the quality of the experience with each interaction.

However, I wanted to also understand from Skander how trust was built regarding risk management and regulatory compliance in the highly complex financial services industry. Skander explained that a decentralised structure is in place, with an experienced senior compliance leader responsible within each market to ensure OFX stays informed and updated on regulations. Each local compliance leader has responsibility for financial and non-financial metrics.

Invest in technology

Since 2018, OFX has invested over AUD $54 million in CAPEX[12]. As a result of this investment, OFX has continued to scale quickly and safely, delivering excellent client experience while maintaining flat operating expenses.

However, in addition to investments in systems, processes and measurement systems to support the needs of its customers, Skander also shared he invests significantly in employees.

Develop a capable team

I asked Skander how he maintains an engaged and committed team of 715 employees worldwide. He shared that to achieve outstanding client results and a consistently high net promoter score, investing in the professional development of his team is essential. I also learned that Skander's focus and genuine commitment to environmental, social and governance (ESG) are crucial to attracting and retaining staff.

During our conversation, Skander also revealed an interesting approach to recruitment. Given the time zone challenges, he understands that working for a global company is not for everybody. He explained that as a 24/7 business, it was not unusual for meetings to occur outside standard business hours, which can impact personal family time. Skander appreciated that while this 'comes with the territory', not everybody wants this.

Skander also shared that his first requirement when recruiting executives and board members is that they must all have global experience – they must embrace and understand from first-hand experience the idea that every market is different. In addition, all global leaders must project confidence, authenticity and a desire to maintain solid local market connections to make sense of the world and understand how to engage with clients.

OFX's agility as a culture and work environment means it can quickly modify its business processes to provide exceptional products and services to clients. It is highly adaptable and offers in-market brand and market strategies to support clients at every local level.

OFX is a global expansion success story. It represents what is possible, especially with a strong customer focus, investment in technology and support for the professional development of staff. What is also interesting is that the factors discussed by Skander also align with the characteristics of successful global companies discussed earlier in this chapter.

***

Venice and Genoa were competing maritime Republics. Their future prosperity and survival depended on trade, and they competed to monopolise the best trading routes and secure the finest products. However, their entrepreneurs were the common thread that bound them together. Polo travelled to the other side of the world to observe people and lived with them to understand their culture and customs. It was from this experience that he understood their unique ways, and built his business around that reality. More broadly, it was also from this entrepreneurial mindset that, despite the heady days of Venetian and Genovese trading dominance being long gone, their impact on the modern-day financial services industry remains significant. They developed payment instruments to facilitate transactions, revolutionised international trade and paved the way for modern-day political, cultural and economic globalisation. The importance of Venice and Genoa as the revolutionaries of global trade has perhaps been lost over the centuries, but we continue to see their impact today in many corners of the world.

Top 5 insights from this chapter

1. The merchants of Venice paved the way for globalisation with their private banks. They established Bancogiro, the first European national bank regulating secure financial passage and trade for valuable goods.

2. Securing international trade is achieved with a foundation based on a regulated system, with today's companies leveraging new technologies to facilitate cross-border transactions.

3. Successful global businesses often attribute their success to employees with lived international business experience from target markets.

4. Characteristics of global companies are important for early-stage scaleups to consider as they plan their growth into new markets.

5. Listening to the customer, building trust, investing in technology and developing a capable team are the four pillars of success for OFX.

APPLYING LEARNINGS TO YOUR BUSINESS

Self-reflection: Consider the characteristics of global companies as discussed. Does your business represent these characteristics? How could you develop in certain areas?

CHAPTER 3

CONSIDERING THE JOURNEY AHEAD

We need to accept that we won't always make the right decisions, that we'll screw up royally sometimes – understanding that failure is not the opposite of success, it's part of success.

Arianna Huffington, co-founder of *The Huffington Post*

In this chapter I address an important concept fundamental to your business's growth success – the Business Growth Lifecycle. I developed this concept after researching a framework to guide my own business. While many models were already available, they either included components that were irrelevant or left out elements that seemed important when it came to my own business. I wanted a simple chart with a clear algorithm that tied together the lifecycles of businesses and outlined the transitional phases as they grow and expand into new markets.

Each phase of the Business Growth Lifecycle comes with its own set of challenges. As a leader looking to expand globally, you need to understand the internal and external forces that come to bear in each phase and be prepared to overcome the challenges that will inevitably arise.

This fact gives rise to a cluster of critical questions:

- 'Which stage of the business lifecycle is my company at?'

- 'What are the characteristics of each stage?'
- 'What are the critical business challenges and focus areas I need to know?'
- 'What measures do I track, and when?'

In this chapter, I provide answers to these questions.

The Business Growth Lifecycle

Before diving into the specifics of the Business Growth Lifecycle, let me quickly explain that various approaches can be used to describe a business's life stages, based on aspects such as timeframe or revenue. For simplicity, I have included the timeframe (the number of years) in business and captured the characteristics that typically define each phase. However, while 'timeframe' is part of the approach I have used, what is more important is to choose the stage relevant to your business (such as 'scaleup' or 'growth') and then read about the characteristics that apply.

The following figure shows the main stages in my Business Growth Lifecycle, as a business moves from prototype to maturity. You can see in the figure that I have also highlighted the four main foundations of a business – leadership, governance, funding and process management – and how these change at each stage of the business cycle. In the following sections, I provide an overview of the main stages in the business cycle and the evolution of the four foundations. The chapters in part II cover the four foundational areas in much more detail – see chapter 4 for more on entrepreneurial leadership characteristics, chapter 5 for governance, chapter 6 for pitching for funding and chapter 7 for process management.

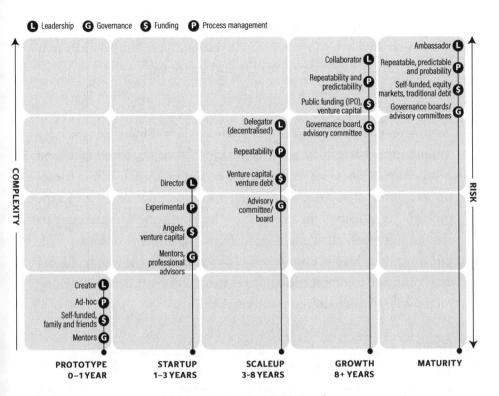

Ambassador **L**

Collaborator **L**   Repeatable, predictable and probability **P**

Repeatability and predictability **P**

Self-funded, equity markets, traditional debt **S**

Public funding (IPO), venture capital **S**

Governance boards/ advisory committees **G**

Delegator (decentralised) **L**

Governance board, advisory committee **G**

Repeatability **P**

Venture capital, venture debt **S**

Director **L**

Advisory committee/ board **G**

Experimental **P**

Angels, venture capital **S**

Mentors, professional advisors **G**

Creator **L**

Ad-hoc **P**

Self-funded, family and friends **S**

Mentors **G**

COMPLEXITY   RISK

| PROTOTYPE 0–1 YEAR | STARTUP 1–3 YEARS | SCALEUP 3–8 YEARS | GROWTH 8+ YEARS | MATURITY |

The Business Growth Lifecycle

Prototype (0–1 year)

When developing a prototype, entrepreneurs often use a process known as 'design thinking', and this process starts with clearly articulating the problem to be solved. This is a proven methodology to help define and build a solution – the prototype – for the end users. Design thinking requires deep research to empathise with the end user, clearly define the problem, ideate a solution, build a prototype and test the design of the solution. A powerful benefit of design thinking is that it allows entrepreneurs to adjust at any stage of the process to incorporate learnings – that is, it is not a linear method.

Confusion often emerges about the difference between design thinking and user experience (UX) design. Both methodologies are based on understanding the end user's problem and can be used in conjunction. In my experience, design thinking starts with a problem, whereas UX design starts with a solution (the prototype), using human-centred behavioural research, tests and retesting to ultimately design a product that is easy for the end customer.

Challenges

At this very early stage in the lifecycle of the business, generating a unique idea that can be transformed into a viable, sustainable and prosperous business isn't easy (as you no doubt know). While there's no guarantee of success, developing a unique solution to a specific problem is possible. In contrast, I have observed entrepreneurs risk failing when their ideological frame of mind is obsessed with pursuing their idea – even when it's solving a problem that doesn't exist or is not common enough to matter. Using the design thinking methodology can help you avoid this pitfall.

Focus

To successfully guide your business through this lifecycle stage, you should consider educating yourself or securing an expert in design thinking or UX design before attempting to define the user experience and ultimately design and test solutions. These methodologies require specific skill sets, and only by applying this knowledge will you obtain the best result for your efforts.

Leadership

Founders are driven by their ability to combine creativity and motivation to solve a specific problem. They have a steadfast commitment to, and confidence in, their desire to achieve their vision. The leader's function at this stage is to build a prototype, then test and retest. This, along with their predisposition as a risk-taker, defines the leader as an experimenter and creator at this stage of the business lifecycle. On a practical level, founders leverage their existing skills and experience – or secure an expert, as discussed earlier – and follow specific methodologies to identify the problem they are passionate about solving and create a prototype.

At this stage of the lifecycle, leaders have high energy and are focused on experimenting with their user-centred designs. Leaders must have an unwavering focus on the end-user, combined with questioning, creativity and critical thinking to uncover their future customers' needs.

Governance

Perhaps you're surprised to encounter 'governance' at this formative stage of the Business Growth Lifecycle. As a governance professional, I believe the earlier entrepreneurs understand governance, risk management and compliance principles, the better placed they are to identify and manage this as the business progresses and matures.

At this stage of the business lifecycle, some entrepreneurs prefer to validate and test their prototypes before formalising business structures. However, others prefer to secure their business name and register it with the appropriate regulator. This important step is often the first interaction entrepreneurs have with a regulator, and, from that point on, they are formally bound by the laws and obligations of the jurisdiction in which they operate. For example, in Australia, you must be 18 years of age to register a company name and secure an Australian Business Number (ABN). You must also consent to take on the roles and responsibilities of a director and apply for a Director Identification Number (Director ID). This then means the entity (and, therefore, the director) is governed by the *Corporations Act (2001)*, and securing director's and officer's liability insurance becomes essential.

Funding

Entrepreneurs use several approaches to secure funding at this prototype stage of the business lifecycle. What is most popular is 'bootstrapping', where entrepreneurs use their own funds to start the business (which also reflects their risk-taking abilities). Other approaches are to seek early-stage private investors, who are often friends or family.

Some entrepreneurs raising capital at this stage may consider crowdfunding as their first strategy. However, crowdfunding is highly specialised and to be successful, a significant level of planning is essential. Recruiting an experienced crowdfunding specialist will be important to execute and achieve the desired results.

A successful crowdfunding campaign was run by an Australian company called Flow Hive – a beehive business that designed a unique frame that allows honey extraction without needing to open the beehive. In just eight weeks, Flow Hive raised approximately USD \$12 million. The success of this campaign was due to deep research to understand their target market and capture the key messages to those audiences. Their clever marketing campaign included a strong environmental message regarding the importance of bees to communities. Critically, they also targeted innovators – that is, those within their social networks who were at the forefront of new product development. Crowdfunding is not for everyone, though, and some businesses, even in this early stage, prefer to secure 'angel' investors (see 'Funding' in the next section).

Processes

Design thinking and UX design require entrepreneurs to map the processes that make up the prototype. In addition, at this early stage, establishing a process to capture feedback from user testing is essential and will inform future end-user designs. This often takes the form of a 'landing page', specifically created to capture and register details of users testing the prototype.

Startup (1–3 years in business)

Once the prototype has been tested and validated to solve the end-user problem, the business typically transitions into the second stage of the Business Growth Lifecycle – the startup phase. The focus is on building the minimum viable product (MVP), identifying the unique value proposition (UVP), building brand awareness, and selling the product or service.

Challenges

Governments around the globe recognise and, to a greater or lesser extent, support the economic powerhouse of startups by offering grants and tax incentives, and removing regulatory barriers. However, the following statistics are a reminder that the startup phase represents the highest risk of failure in the business lifecycle:

- In Australia, 20 per cent of companies fail in their first year, with approximately 60 per cent failing in the first three years.[1]

- In the United States, 0.5 per cent or 1 out of 200 new companies will reach the scaleup phase. According to the United States Bureau of Labor Statistics, the odds are stacked against startups, with 90 per cent failing over the long term. Of the startups that survive the first year, only 50 per cent will make it to their fifth year.

- In the United Kingdom, approximately 80 per cent of companies fail within their first year and, according to the UK Office for National Statistics, for businesses that started in 2013, only 42.4 per cent were still trading five years later.

Research further shows that startups fail at this early stage due to several factors – including a lack of market knowledge, lack of product and customer (preliminary) validation, unfit employees, lack of funds and ineffective marketing. The key to successfully navigating this stage is to keep these potential hurdles in mind and activate remediation strategies as soon as weaknesses become apparent.

However, another key challenge is time in the market. Due to the innovative nature of their solution, founders can spend significant time explaining the solution and educating industry colleagues on the problem they are solving, and outlining their research and market insights that have influenced this solution. This often results in the founder spending considerably more time than they have available to close partnership or sales deals. As a global mentor, I have observed that this challenge is more common in Australia than in the United States or the United Kingdom due to external factors such as market maturity and cultural factors such as risk tolerance and openness to new ideas. However, this challenge in educating the market can also highlight new insights, requiring founders to pivot to new product features, or an entirely new market segment.

Focus

To ensure that your business doesn't become one of the 90 per cent of businesses that don't make it, you need to focus on the following critical tasks:

- securing funding
- defining your business model
- defining your unique value proposition (UVP)
- building and testing your minimum viable product (MVP)
- recruiting and building your team.

I cover startup funding separately later in this chapter, and provide more detail on the other four tasks in the following section. With these tasks complete, the focus becomes building brand awareness, and selling the product or service.

Defining your business model

A tool entrepreneurs and leaders use at this startup phase is the Business Model Canvas, developed by Alex Osterwalder. He identified and emphasised the importance of nine fundamental attributes for entrepreneurs to identify for their prototypes as they enter the startup phase. Comprehensive instructions on how to apply the model to your business can be found in Osterwalder's bestselling 2010 book, *Business Model Generation*.

Defining your unique value proposition

After defining your business model, the next step is to consider what makes your idea different from other products in the market. For example, consider a ride-hailing company like Uber. If you were considering starting a business in this industry, you would need to ask yourself, 'Why would people use my product if an established known brand already offers the same service?' This is where your unique value proposition (UVP) or unique selling proposition comes in. According to entrepreneur.com's *Small Business Encyclopedia*, a unique selling proposition is the 'factor or consideration presented by a seller as the reason that one product or service is different from and better than that of the competition'.[2] In other words, using Uber again as an example, your UVP should answer, 'What do I do that is unique from Uber?' For example, you may introduce cheaper fares, guarantee safer rides, or offer a service for a specific market segment.

Defining your UVP is often one of the biggest challenges for start-ups. The Value Proposition Canvas, developed by Peter J Thomson, is a tool available to assist entrepreneurs with this process. This tool combines behavioural research and design thinking, and requires you to determine where your products intersect with your customers' desires.[3]

Defining your minimum viable product

Frank Robinson introduced the concept of a minimum viable product (MVP) as part of his Lean Startup methodology, which can be found in his popular book *The Lean Startup*. He defines MVP as 'the version of a new product that allows a team to collect the maximum amount of validated learning about customers with the least amount of effort'.

The lean methodology calls for entrepreneurs to experiment, test, gather customer feedback and then iterate products early on based on the insights gained in the process, rather than spending months trying to perfect a product or service before launching. This method aims to shorten the time between developing and delivering a product so that entrepreneurs can discover if their business model (based at this point only on assumptions and hypotheses) is feasible. At this early stage, I have seen entrepreneurs create a website 'landing page' with basic information to capture the details of those registering to receive launch updates. This has proven valuable from a marketing perspective, with a ready-made subscriber list available when the business moves into the next phase.

The Lean Startup methodology has also adopted concepts from the agile approach, often used in project management and software development. The agile approach develops a product prototype and launches it into the market to get feedback without wasting unnecessary time or resources on refining something that hasn't been tested in the real world. The Lean Startup methodology similarly focuses heavily on the build-measure-learn (BML) process.

Several years ago, I attended a webinar with a client presenting their latest software release to a prospect. My client was using the BML process, and as the demo proceeded, the prospect asked for additional fields to be added to the software. As the prospect shared their requirements, my client's developer updated and showed the changes on the screen and in real-time. This was a powerful example of applying changes to software using the BML process.

Another example of a business that has used the lean methodology is the cloud-based file transfer service Dropbox. Dropbox started as an MVP – in the form of a three-minute video showing people what it could do. The objective was to test whether demand existed for the product while creating an audience of potential users. The feedback received through this strategy helped shape the product, and today Dropbox has more than 700 million users worldwide.

You can read further insights about Dropbox's story in chapter 11.

Recruiting your team

Another challenge at this phase is recruiting, onboarding and retaining the right talent. Recruiting for the right knowledge, skills and motivations is important; however, it's also essential to ensure recruits can work in the fast-paced culture of a scaleup. According to Startup Nation, in the United States the staff turnover rate for startups is approximately 25 per cent, almost double the national average of 13 per cent.[4]

In addition, while recruiting for the right fit is important, offering appropriate benefits, onboarding, and retention initiatives are essential.

Leadership

Leaders leverage their existing skills and experience to direct staff to develop a solution to achieve their vision at this stage in the business cycle. Leaders are highly motivated, energetic and focused on experimenting with their business model attributes and validating the UVP. These attributes are why I define leaders as being the 'director' at this stage.

Startup leaders often leverage their creative and entrepreneur abilities to solve problems quickly; however, as the weight of funding pressures increases, it's not uncommon for their communication style to become increasingly direct. While leaders at this early stage have many roles, sales and fundraising often become their primary responsibility. The challenge, however, is that while their focus is on these two critical tasks, they require support to ensure other functions in the business continue. To be effective, the startup leader requires a well-developed and unique set of interpersonal skills.

As a mentor to startups, the skills in the following areas are what I believe are critical:

- identifying and managing the important fundamentals – financials, operations and risk – by either obtaining external assistance or internal hiring
- establishing a clear vision, and communicating it regularly to inspire the team, clients and other critical stakeholders
- establishing, and communicating regularly, realistic goals and strategies for individual team members to achieve them
- creating a healthy culture where the team can thrive and contribute to the growth of the business
- formulating basic policies to operationalise the core functions in the business, and assigning responsibilities of team members
- recognising and developing basic policies to effectively respond to environmental, sustainability and governance principles.

Startups are high-risk, and learning from failure is core to establishing a learning culture, and achieving ultimate success. As a leader at this stage, establishing 'client listening posts' to obtain ongoing feedback is crucial. Engaging with the social media channels and other communities your clients participate in is also essential.

Governance

At this stage of the Business Growth Lifecycle, mentors are crucial in adding value to startups by providing guidance and expertise to entrepreneurs navigating the challenging landscape of building a new business. In my experience, mentors contribute to the success of startups by bringing their experience, network and connections, and offering constructive feedback. Also, mentors offer emotional support and encouragement during the highs and lows that entrepreneurs inevitably experience along the way.

Entrepreneurs should ensure they select mentors who align to their business needs. For example, in a highly regulated industry, mentors with risk management expertise are often a valuable source of guidance to help navigate compliance complexities.

Associating with a respected mentor can also enhance a startup's credibility and reputation. The mentor's endorsement can instil confidence in potential investors, customers and partners, opening up opportunities for growth and success. Their guidance and contributions can be instrumental in increasing the likelihood of success for early-stage ventures.

Funding

At this stage, startups may look to 'angel' investors. These private investors provide financial support to kick-start a business in exchange for an equity stake. In many cases, the angel investor offers a one-time investment. If there are early signs of success, they may make ongoing investments throughout the business lifecycle.

Providing the startup has tested its product or service and has secured clients, it can move towards the 'seed round' of funding. Typically, the seed round consists of investments in which 15 or fewer investors typically contribute between AUD $25,000 and

AUD $2 million to the business – known as 'venture capital'. This funding generally helps with initial market research, team member hiring and MVP development. While it's not the norm, startups can participate in more than one seed round.

A company with the potential to grow and generate revenue typically moves from seed towards 'series A' funding. This generally entails an investment of anywhere between AUD $2 million and AUD $10 million by angel investors or venture capitalists in exchange for preferred shares in the company. The main goal of a series A round is to invest in the company to support expansion by hiring more skilled workers and investing further in product development.

Processes

At this startup stage of the Business Growth Lifecycle, processes are rarely documented, and standardised workflows are rarely adhered to – with a flurry of activity, experimentation and pivoting instead taking place. However, as the product design starts to take shape, two processes typically receive the greatest attention at this stage:

- managing financials – that is, watching the cash burn rate
- using customer feedback to validate the minimum viable product.

Startups at this stage must not neglect the more mundane yet critical business of identifying basic core processes and establishing a high degree of standardisation. This is especially important during the later years of the startup phase, when raising capital becomes the primary focus. It is not unusual for investors, especially venture capitalists, to request operational documentation as part of their due diligence. Process standardisation is a laborious yet necessary task for startups, and I discuss this process in much more detail in chapter 7.

Embedding discipline on process documentation is essential for another reason. As discussed, staff turnover can be high at this phase and, therefore, knowledge, relationships and ways of working are at risk if there is no process management. For example, consider if a sales representative resigns. What are the implications? Do you have a process that captures their sales pipelines, prospect proposals and client contracts? These are just some questions to consider with process management.

A common phrase by entrepreneurs is 'think global from the start'. A crucial factor in global success is identifying and managing core processes by assigning ownership, tracking outcomes and creating a learning environment to empower teams to identify shortcomings and opportunities and act on them promptly. These are fundamentally important at this stage and will shore up global expansion opportunities.

Scaleup (3–8+ years in business)

The next stage in the business cycle is scaling up. This is when businesses typically start thinking about expanding into global markets, and it's when many business leaders seek my advice. It's natural for organisations to want to grow and increase their revenue, but this growth often requires additional resources. What sets a scaleup apart from a regular business is its ability to increase revenue without incurring extra costs and resources. Another factor distinguishing a scaleup from a startup is achieving an annual growth rate of 20 per cent for at least three years and having a minimum of 10 employees. While this isn't an absolute rule, it should be a guiding principle for leaders when considering global growth objectives.

Challenges

One of the first challenges founders face in this stage is determining the right time to scale. Scaling too early can spell disaster for a startup and many fail because they try to scale up too quickly. I wrote this book with the intention of helping scaleups avoid such a high failure rate. One common reason for this failure is that founders mistakenly believe that scaling is the driving force behind development when, in reality, growth drives scaling, not the other way around.

In addition to understanding when to scale, founders may encounter another issue that creates tension within their team during this critical stage. As the business expands and enters new markets, an effective strategy is to partner with an established, mature corporation. However, a disconnect can quickly arise between the founder's fast-paced approach and the often slower rhythm of these established companies. Leaders from both organisations must be aware of this tension, ensure they align their expectations for delivery with potential partners, and be prepared to adapt and make changes accordingly.

The scaleup phase of the lifecycle also represents challenges in staff recruitment and retention. Leaders need to ensure their workforce plan is in line with their growth strategy; that is, the right people are in critical roles at the right time to support this phase of growth. Resilience, employee motivation and a genuine commitment to the company's purpose are all critical measurements of managing staff turnover. In addition, offering employee stock options (ESOP) can also be an effective method to motivate and retain highly skilled and experienced staff in critical roles, and build team spirit and commitment. Research also highlights that by offering ESOP, scaleup rates are significantly increased.[5]

Focus

The primary focus at this stage is generating sales and building a client base beyond the early adopters. Increasing revenue with acute attention to profitability is critical, and why the appointment of a sales leader is a vital step – as is continuing to build the internal infrastructure to scale. This includes recruiting talented people for functional roles across customer support and marketing. This can also mean recruiting offshore leaders to drive focus, build brand awareness and obtain market intelligence from target clients.

Leadership

Theoretical physicist John Wheeler was a later collaborator of Albert Einstein. He described Einstein's approach as follows: 'Out of clutter, find simplicity, from discord make harmony, and in the middle of difficulty lies opportunity.' This is the approach leaders need to keep in mind as they move into the scaleup stage.

One of the most daunting tasks for many leaders at this stage is the commitment to lead their venture's transformation from a single-market operation to a multi-market business. I often witness leaders stepping down from their positions during this critical growth stage due to the overwhelming nature of this transition.

It is imperative for leaders to cultivate trust within their teams by mastering the art of delegation. As the business grows, leaders are increasingly challenged to maintain their involvement in the operational aspects they once handled. Consequently, acquiring fresh leadership skills, especially delegation, is most impactful when staff members are granted authority and held accountable for jointly established objectives. Founders, in particular, often encounter difficulties in delegating tasks effectively. Nevertheless, founders and newly onboarded team members assigned to specific responsibilities can face adverse consequences if founders continue to micromanage, potentially leading to the departure of these team members.

Let's look at precisely what challenges a leader will be facing here. With a leadership team in place, the leader's style must balance the need for 'control' with 'delegation'. That sounds simple enough, but this is often where things go awry. As mentioned, trust is the cornerstone of effective delegation, but as Jim Collins explains in his book *BE 2.0 (Beyond Entrepreneurship): Turning Your Business into an Enduring Great Company*,

> Trust is only one side of the coin. The other side is rigorous standards. There are two parts to this: values standards and performance standards. Values standards are the most rigid. If someone disregards your company's core values, they should be asked to leave. If they understand and disrespect any of your sacred tenets, they don't belong ... Performance standards should be less rigid, but very high. Good performers

lose respect for companies that tolerate poor performance. However, remember that there may be many causes for poor performance.

To establish a delegation process, I recommend that leaders use a delegation matrix to establish clear lines of roles and responsibilities for staff. This matrix helps functional managers fully comprehend their duties and the extent of their decision-making authority, ensuring that roles are clearly defined. Simultaneously, the matrix gives leaders the confidence that the business will continue to grow within established guidelines.

Governance

During the scaleup stage, I have observed various strategies adopted by founders to ensure they effectively manage risk and comply with industry regulations. Employing a full-time chief risk officer is not always financially feasible; however, in highly regulated industries, securing a compliance specialist on a contractual basis is often the chosen alternative.

However, founders should also consider establishing an advisory committee, also known as an advisory board or advisory council. The committee typically consists of individuals who have previous involvement in the business, including mentors with governance experience.

Appointing advisory committee members requires careful consideration, taking into account their relevant skillset, and knowledge they can contribute to guide the business. It is also essential to establish whether or not advisory committee members have a fiduciary responsibility towards the company. As they consider establishing their governance structure, founders often ask me if advisory committee members with fiduciary responsibility should be compensated. Unfortunately, no straightforward answer to this question is possible. However, as a general guideline, advisory committee members can receive equity ranging from 0.5 to 5 per cent, depending on their level of expertise and the contributions they are expected to make. For example, those at the lower end of the equity range may be expected to attend four advisory committee meetings per year and provide four introductions to their network.

Funding

When a company reaches the scaleup stage, a primary objective is long-term growth by increasing market share and profitability. To achieve this, scaleups often need to raise capital, commonly through a series A funding round. As the business expands into global markets, the need for additional capital becomes even more pronounced, often leading to a second series A round or a series B round. These rounds can be secured through venture capital or venture debt. However, it's important to note that raising capital at this stage can be more challenging due to the higher stakes involved.

Processes

At the scaleup stage, you should be aiming for process repeatability within your business. For example, even when I founded FD Global Connections in 2014, I always intended to build an international business. I worked across the Australian and the US markets from the beginning, so every task I undertook was with a global mindset. At that time, I implemented the essentials first – such as financial software and desktop tools to create templates, proposals and marketing strategy, including brand positioning. However, I knew that at some stage, the business would outgrow my capacity to manage the day-to-day running effectively. Over time and with capital generated from the business, I have deployed software to allow me to focus on supporting clients with their global expansion strategies while my processes remain intact. Today, I have process automation across my business, including artificial intelligence (AI) products as follows:

- Financial management software gives me real-time financial statements and invoicing.

- A client relationship management (CRM) system helps me manage sales and client engagement, with an all-important 'task reminder' function and integration into my financial management software.
- An AI-driven virtual assistant manages my calendar, liaising online and directly with customers, including providing meeting reminders and rescheduling options.
- An AI note taker captures notes and actions from meetings and webinars.

When clients ask me that critical question, 'Is my business ready to expand internationally?', we first undertake an audit to determine whether the technology is in place to support global processes.

Earlier in the chapter, I emphasised the importance of establishing discipline and laying a solid foundation for managing your core processes of a startup. As you progress into the scaleup phase of the business cycle, it becomes crucial to demonstrate maturity in process management before moving forward. This entails identifying the top five business processes, assigning ownership, documenting them, measuring performance and communicating outcomes. By this stage, financials and culture are usually being effectively managed; however, as a scaleup, attention turns to three core processes: sales, client support/operations and marketing functions. These critical processes should be well-defined, and be repeatable with predictable results.

Effective process management plays a vital role in controlling workflows. It leads to fewer operational errors and reduced overall expenses, and provides insights into opportunities for improving efficiency. Drawing from my extensive experience, I can confidently state that a scaleup expanding into a new market without proper management of its core processes is at a significantly higher risk of failure.

Growth (8+ years)

During the growth stage, a company aims to establish a strong foothold in the industry, expand its market share and boost its profitability. By this point, customer relationships have typically surpassed the three- or four-year mark, resulting in referrals and a positive net promoter score. Resources such as workspace and the number of employees are expanded to accommodate the growing demands of the business.

Challenges

A growing business brings numerous significant challenges, such as workload management, compliance, intense competition, and managing diverse and potentially conflicting customer needs.

One specific challenge I have observed in working with leaders and their teams, especially those involved in all previous stages of building the business up to this point in the lifecycle, is fatigue. Fatigue is a sign of burnout and stress, and according to a study from Gartner, employees' ability to cope with stress is 50 per cent lower than what it was before the pandemic.[6] The Gartner study offered two solutions to better absorb change:

- *Build trust:* Ensure employees believe that their leaders and Human Resources (HR) have their best interests in mind, consider the impact the change will have, and say what you mean and follow through on promises. According to Gartner, employees who have higher trust in the change effort have 2.6 times the capacity to absorb changes compared to those with low trust.

- *Improve team cohesion:* Ensure team members share a sense of belonging, connection and commitment to, and accountability for, a collective goal. Employees with strong team cohesion have a capacity for change 1.8 times greater than the capacity of those with low team cohesion.

Focus

Increasing market share is a core focus for this stage of the Business Growth Lifecycle. However, a critical challenge to a company's growth is introducing new products to meet ever-increasing client demands while winning sales to generate capital. In addition, as the company grows, its compliance responsibilities increase, and meeting the rules and regulations across several jurisdictions is necessary for its long-term viability.

Leadership

At this stage, founders and leaders are reaping the rewards of laying the proper foundations to build and support a positive and highly effective culture during the startup and scaleup phases. Defining the purpose, vision and values in those formative years is fundamental to the ongoing reputation and success of the company. The kind of culture I am referring to here is one built on a clarity of purpose, and the leadership style at this stage is marked by collaboration, trust and respect, where equality, diversity and creativity are embedded in the fabric of the organisation. If an investment in culture did not occur during the early stages of the business, high staff turnover, poor client experiences and an uncertain outcome when it comes to shareholder returns will emerge at this stage.

The irony is that many leaders believe the growth stage requires the highest degree of control on their part. However, in my experience, the opposite is true. This is the phase where the leader becomes a collaborator. As collaborators, leaders support and empower staff to be productive in the roles they've been recruited for. This may sound a little counterintuitive, but if you think about the history of successful businesses at this stage of the business lifecycle, their success can be put down to their ability to pivot, to develop creative solutions to problems, to delegate effectively and to operate with agility. This comes not from controlling staff but through empowering them.

Governance

At this lifecycle stage, considerable focus and attention is essential to ensure effective and regular oversight of governance, compliance and risk management. Leaders must assess the most effective structure – for example, expanding their existing advisory committee with representation from the new market, or formalising a governance board. In some markets, regulations require a governance board, especially in highly regulated industries such as financial services and health.

Funding

A business is in the growth phase when it has established itself in at least one market and continues to access new markets, make acquisitions and develop new products. From the point of view of funding at this stage, companies will be utilising working capital or raising the required funds through traditional debt, private equity or public markets via listing on the stock exchange.

Processes

At this stage, the business needs to have a comprehensive understanding of its core business processes. I previously highlighted the importance of establishing measurement systems for the top five processes during the scaleup phase. The effectiveness of these systems will become apparent in the growth stage. If a business has successfully implemented tracking and measurement systems during the scaleup phase, the emphasis will now be on enhancing the predictability of financial outcomes.

Maturity

There is absolutely no innovation without failure.
Brené Brown

In the previous stages, the company aimed to focus on long-term growth. In the maturity stage, the primary goal is to fortify its market position. As a business matures, sales often decrease, and profit margins get thinner, with the flow of capital becoming stagnant. However, companies that continue to grow steadily are those with a culture of internal innovation and an openness to mergers and acquisitions opportunities.

As the following figure shows, the average lifespan of a company on the S&P 500 is in decline.[7] In the mid-1960s, it was approximately 30 years, compared to fewer than 20 years now. This decline is expected to continue, for the most part, because of the impact of technological changes.

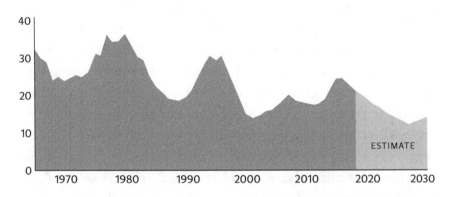

Average company tenure on S&P, years measured as rolling seven-year average[8]

Challenges

A mature business faces many challenges, including competition, maintaining brand presence and identifying new revenue lines. Unless the company can demonstrate its current vision and purpose through refreshed branding or innovative products and services, mature businesses risk being viewed as 'traditional' and 'out of touch'. Therefore, to avoid this, engaging with employees, clients and the broader community on an ongoing basis is vital.

Focus

Unless the founder focuses on creativity and innovation, many businesses start declining once they reach maturity. The businesses that thrive tend to be marked by a culture that invests in the development of their employees and encourages new ideas from all levels across the business.

Leadership

The most significant risk for leaders of mature companies is complacency. 'Too big to fail' is often heralded as a badge of honour but, as history has shown, large, established and respected multinational companies can still fail. Lehman Brothers and Kodak are two examples of highly visible corporate collapses.

The reality is that leaders of global multinational organisations have major hurdles to overcome. They must continually perform at a high level in the face of greater complexity when navigating multiple markets, cultures, regulations and delivering shareholder returns. Success at this level requires significant energy from leaders – and their role transforms from collaborators into ambassadors for their organisation. They must continue injecting positive energy across an organisational culture often spread across multiple jurisdictions, and apportion their time between the need to be internally focused and (even more so) the need to be externally focused on clients, investors and other stakeholders. Balancing these priorities often differentiates those who succeed and those who fail.

Governance

Governance boards are usually developed by this stage of the business cycle; however, it's important to periodically review the company strategy and ensure the skills and experience of board members continue to be aligned to the business. Establishing regular skills assessments of board members and ensuring governance structures are in place that align with current global and industry issues are all essential to maintain relevance.

Funding

Self-funding, equity markets and traditional debt are typical funding options for mature businesses.

Processes

Businesses should have a solid understanding of process management by this stage. Core processes are identified, measurement systems established, and rigour with repeatability, predictability and the probability of process outcomes should be entrenched across the business. (These three elements of repeatability, predictability and probability comprise my Process Scalability Formula, which I discuss in much more detail in chapter 7.) With strong process management, the business should be agile and able to pivot and deploy new technology to address process and product gaps.

As mentioned earlier, the biggest threat at this stage is the risk of complacency. A company where the importance of experimentation is not understood, and the activity itself is not encouraged, is one with an uncertain future.

***

Prince famously said, 'Sometimes it takes years for a person to become an overnight success.' In other words, there is no shortcut to success. Any business takes years of hard work, talent, patience, resilience and teamwork to succeed. The Business Growth Lifecycle highlights the critical phases of companies on a growth trajectory. It is an attempt to provide a pathway for entrepreneurs to see the journey ahead, the challenges they will experience and the risks they may encounter. While the lifecycle is not guaranteed to work out in the same way for every business and may not be linear for some, looking at how to transition from one stage to the next and being prepared for the possible hurdles each step entails can help prepare you and your business for the next stage of growth.

Of course, each journey is unique – as you will see in part II when I dive deeper into the four pillars and explore how CEOs have approached their challenges.

Top 5 insights from this chapter

1. The Business Lifecycle I developed is a broadly applicable framework that can guide your business through transitional phases of global expansion.

2. Regardless of size, all companies experience transitional phases, and each of these comes with its own set of challenges including:
   - leadership
   - governance
   - funding
   - process management.

3. The startup phase represents the highest risk of the business lifecycle. More than 90 per cent of startups fail due to lack of research, unfit employees, lack of funds and ineffective marketing.

4. Premature scaling is considered one of the most common signs of imminent doom for a startup. Around 70 per cent of businesses fail because they scale up too fast.

5. While there is a typical business lifecycle, not all businesses go through the same stages or in the same order. All businesses are different, with some quickly progressing from startup to maturity, and exits can occur at any stage.

Self-reflection: Where is your business in the lifecycle? Are you satisfied you have the plan in place to move to the next stage of the lifecycle?

_____

_____

_____

_____

_____

_____

_____

_____

_____

_____

_____

_____

_____

PART II

LAYING THE FOUNDATIONS FOR GLOBAL GROWTH

Welcome to part II of *Decoding Global Growth*, where we delve deeper into the essential aspects of achieving sustainable growth from the Business Growth Lifecycle. In part I, we laid the groundwork by introducing the lifecycle and emphasising the significance of four foundational elements. Each of these elements – leadership, governance, funding (pitching and storytelling) and process management – is explored in dedicated chapters in this part.

In chapter 4, I explore the critical role of effective leadership in driving growth. I examine the identified qualities that successful entrepreneurs and leaders employ to steer their organisations from early prototype stage towards global expansion. Through the latest research, inspiring examples and practical insights, I outline the key attributes of visionary leaders.

Continuing our journey, chapter 5 sheds light on the vital aspect of establishing robust governance structures within growing organisations. I delve into the principles and practices that enable companies to maintain transparency, accountability and ethical conduct. By examining various governance models and best practices, I also provide guidance on building a strong governance framework to support sustainable growth.

In chapter 6, I consider the art of storytelling as a compelling tool to attract investors, clients and other stakeholders. By examining successful funding stories and sharing practical strategies, I equip you (as an entrepreneur and business leader) with the necessary skills to effectively communicate your vision, value proposition and growth potential.

Chapter 7 brings us to the heart of operational efficiency. Here, I introduce my innovative Process Scalability Formula – an invaluable tool for identifying, analysing and measuring core business processes at each lifecycle stage. I discuss how optimising processes can contribute to sustainable growth, and introduce my Global Scalability Audit, a comprehensive approach for assessing and enhancing process scalability.

Achieving sustainable growth demands meticulous attention to detail, establishing robust structures, controls and metrics, and continually monitoring their effectiveness. Throughout the chapters in this part, I provide fresh perspectives and novel approaches to help growth businesses navigate their path to success. By leveraging the Process Scalability Formula and the Global Scalability Audit, you can unlock the full potential of your core processes and propel your business towards long-term growth and prosperity.

CHAPTER 4

THE LEADERSHIP CHARACTERISTICS OF A GLOBAL ENTREPRENEUR

At the heart of capitalism is creative destruction.

Joseph A Schumpeter, Austrian political economist

Let me take you back to 7 December 2015, when the Australian Prime Minister of the day, Malcolm Turnbull, announced the National Innovation and Science Agenda (NISA). This four-year package of AUD $1.1 billion was intended to encourage 'innovation and enterprise, reward risk-taking, and promote science, maths and computing in schools'. 'Ideas and innovation' was the centrepiece of the agenda, underpinned by great expectations about 'future-proofing' Australia's economic prosperity, jobs and growth. The Prime Minister positioned this as the 'ideas boom' to supersede the 'mining boom'.

The response to this announcement was swift and polarised. On one side, the broader public failed to comprehend the benefits of 'innovation' and 'risk-taking'. The conservative media questioned why the government needed to 'future-proof the economy' when Australia was in its 25th year of consecutive economic growth. Meanwhile, business leaders of mature, successful organisations were also critical because, as far as they were concerned, they had already contributed to the economy by providing jobs and services, despite what they saw as the historical lack of government support. Lobbying from these fronts was substantial, and the Australian Assistant Federal Minister for Innovation lost his seat at the next election, thus ending his parliamentary career.

However, a small segment of the population applauded this shift in the government's focus. These individuals were excited that innovation was finally a national priority. In these ranks, 'risk-taking' was reframed as an opportunity to test an idea, and challenge (or break) traditional policies and processes in the interest of moving forward. The perhaps mysterious and closeted job title of 'entrepreneur' (which had taken a beating after the excesses of the 1980s) had again finally gained credence. Moreover, with the NISA enshrined in law, the government was legally bound to spend the allocated funds to deliver the 24 measures outlined in the Innovation Agenda.

Fast-forward to 2023, when government efforts and financial support continue to be vital. While Australia's lower rankings on global competitiveness can't be ignored, coming in at 19th overall,[1] entrepreneurship is now recognised as essential for a dynamic economy to thrive. In our modern world, entrepreneur leaders create jobs and influence the economy by introducing new, unique products and digitising processes to better serve their clients and communities. They are agile, pivot fast, and engage global innovation ecosystems to learn, develop partnerships and attract more customers. They also need strong leadership skills, which need to evolve as they take their business through the typical cycle discussed in chapter 3.

Many Australian businesses aspire to transition into international markets. In fact, studies show that 66 per cent of Australian online companies cater to international clients.[2] According to the Australian Bureau of Statistics, for the 2022–2023 financial year, Australia's total exports increased by 15.8 per cent to AUD $686 billion.[3]

Technology companies are particularly adept at maintaining a strong international profile. In this space, relative newcomers such as Atlassian, Canva, Culture Amp, and Afterpay (which was acquired by US-based Square for USD $29 billion in 2021) are as familiar to the broader population as the bigger traditional companies such as BHP and Macquarie Bank. What's more, either directly or indirectly via retirement plans, Australians have invested in shares in these modern technology companies alongside established corporate titans.

As the Australian business ecosystem continues to evolve, entrepreneurs have upskilled to challenge norms and solve problems methodically. This has been particularly apparent throughout (and in the aftermath of) the COVID-19 pandemic worldwide. In March 2020, when the World Health Organization declared COVID-19 a global pandemic, at FD Global Connections we quickly learned how to adopt virtual meeting technology. We redesigned a 12-month in-person program, updating all content to deliver the program virtually. And our experience is far from unique.

So let's consider the attributes required to be a successful entrepreneur and business leader in any market. In this chapter, I look more deeply into the typical personality type and mindset of entrepreneurs, and the different leadership skills that are needed as they grow their business, particularly from the startup phase into a scaleup.

Entrepreneurs: Who are they? What makes them tick?

In the late 1700s, French economist Jean-Baptiste Say first coined the word 'entreprendre' which means 'to undertake'. More recently, Oxford University Press has defined an entrepreneur as 'an individual who undertakes to supply a good or service to the market for profit. The entrepreneur will usually invest capital in the business and take on the risks associated with the investment'. Let's dig deeper to consider what kinds of people are likely to succeed in the world of entrepreneurship and business leadership.

Several research studies have identified some correlation between an entrepreneur's personality and their success (or failure). However, if you ask investors what they look for in an entrepreneur, you will likely get a different answer from each investor you ask.

Bearing that in mind, research from the Founder Institute does offer some important insights into the qualities and personality traits that predispose some people to be successful entrepreneurs.

The Founder Institute's Entrepreneurial DNA

The Founder Institute is the world's largest pre-seed startup accelerator, supporting more than 7000 entrepreneurs globally since its inception in 2009. Adeo Ressi is the co-founder and chairman of the Founder Institute, who I met during an entrepreneurial study tour to Silicon Valley in 2016. At the time, he was living and working in the world-famous heartland of technological innovation. I was fortunate that Ressi provided insights into his viewpoints regarding entrepreneurs and, in discussions with me, referenced the Entrepreneurial DNA Assessment. This gave me the impetus to further explore the specific personality traits of successful entrepreneurs.

The Founder Institute's Entrepreneurial DNA Assessment began as a hiring 'test' for startup employees in the mid-2000s. Ressi was trying to find the best hires for a fast-paced, venture-backed technology startup in New York City called Gametrust. To do so, he engaged a renowned clinical psychologist to develop an online assessment to screen job applicants and help identify those who would be a culture fit at a company that prioritised aggressive growth goals and constant iteration. This first test focused on IQ and the Big 5 personality traits and was instrumental in several key hires.

When Ressi and Jonathan Greechan created the Founder Institute in 2009, they engaged this same clinical psychologist with a simple question: if an online test was able to identify the right people to *work* at a startup, then could a new test be designed to identify the right people to *start* a startup? They hypothesised that an objective test could predict the likelihood that any person could build a successful technology company – regardless of location, profession, race or demographic. Such a test could scale the evaluation of idea-stage entrepreneurs by removing subjectivity. This was particularly interesting to the Founder Institute – a unique accelerator that works with entrepreneurs at the pure idea stage, where objective data is mostly non-existent.

Originally, the Founder Institute used as its base the already established 'Big 5' personality traits – extraversion, agreeableness, some emotional control (defined as low-range neuroticism), openness and conscientiousness. To this, we can add additional concepts, such as IQ and fluid intelligence. Interestingly, the Founder Institute also identified several traits that limit entrepreneurs – including overt emotional instability, excuse-making, predatory aggressiveness, deceit and narcissism. These may be seen or interpreted as entrepreneurs having delusions regarding their own capabilities and the performance of their business. Interestingly, as their research developed, they found no predictive correlation between IQ and founder success and, therefore, removed IQ from future assessments of entrepreneurial profiling. (This will perhaps be reassuring to business owners who failed advanced mathematics at school!)

A core element of the Institute's research is to define 'success'. During the most recent review of its assessment process, the team collaborated with social scientists and defined success as follows:

> To quickly execute the strategy and short-term goals. Depending on their specific business and goals, metrics such as revenue, adoption, profitability, capital raised, recruitment of top talent, product milestones achieved, and more can all be factored into determining their relative level of success.

I spoke with Megan Todd, Head of Pipeline at Founder Institute, about their most recent research and whether it revealed new insights. Megan explained that her team applied over 2 million data points from 250,000 individuals who had completed the assessment across 126 countries. In addition, they had also undertaken a review of academic research on entrepreneurship. Through this exhaustive and intensive research phase, they found the following:

- There were 15 higher-order personality dimensions and 44 sub-dimensions associated with entrepreneurship. Each dimension captures testing and performance data from 2009, peer-reviewed research, or both.

- All traits were mapped to the Big 5 dimensions to correlate the Founder Institute's previous iterations and results with the oldest versions of the assessment. Several more personality traits – including innovativeness, proactivity and adaptability – were shown to be relevant to entrepreneur success.

Interestingly, 'success' was redefined as revenue growth, employment growth or long-term business survival.

Megan also shared that success was classified into early versus later startup success. Research showed that entrepreneur personality traits such as motivation, confidence and risk-taking predicted early-stage (prototype/seed round) success, measured by first sales revenues, but not longer-term business survival.

However, in the later, mature phases of startup (series A) companies, research showed that entrepreneurs who scored high on risk-taking and motivation continued to attain higher revenues than those who scored low on these traits.

Megan explained that the Institute's understanding of entrepreneur traits and its definition of success continues to evolve. Her team recently completed the 2022 full-year assessment results, and she shared that their definition of 'success' has again broadened. This now includes metrics such as completion of the Founder Institute accelerator, ratings within the program, successful fundraising, revenue growth and company survival rate.

From my discussion with Megan, I also discovered that no single trait specifically defines an entrepreneur. However, the founder must have self-awareness or insight into their abilities and limitations, and secure a co-founder or a leadership team that complements those traits. For example, if the founder has strong competence in sales and is not operational, their recruitment strategy should be to secure a co-founder with operational expertise.

In addition, the business lifecycle stage influences the most important personality traits. The latest research revealed that it is preferred, but not essential, that founders have the following five traits to be successful as they build their prototype, validate their unique value proposition (UVP) and move into the startup stage:

- *Fluid intelligence:* Fluid intelligence refers to the ability of an individual to reason, think flexibly and understand abstract relationships between things. This trait is valuable in leadership and entrepreneurship because it enables entrepreneurs to adapt to changing circumstances, develop innovative solutions, and make connections between seemingly unrelated concepts. Entrepreneurs with high fluid intelligence are often quick learners, can solve complex problems efficiently and possess strong analytical skills.

- *Emotional control:* Emotional control refers to an individual's ability to regulate and manage their emotions effectively. Successful entrepreneurs must navigate various challenges and uncertainties in their journey, and emotional control plays a crucial role in their ability to handle stress, setbacks and failures. Entrepreneurs and leaders with strong emotional control can stay calm and composed under pressure, make rational decisions and maintain focus on their goals. This trait helps them avoid impulsive reactions and make well-informed choices.

- *Autonomy:* Autonomy refers to the ability to be self-directed and hold oneself accountable. Successful entrepreneurs often need to work independently, set goals and take responsibility for their actions. They possess a strong sense of self-motivation and drive, which allows them to stay focused and committed to their vision. Autonomy also means confidence to make decisions and take risks without constant external validation. Entrepreneurs with high autonomy are self-starters who can efficiently manage their time, prioritise tasks and persevere through challenges.

- *Reflection:* Reflection is a trait that correlates strongly with conscientiousness, one of the Big 5 personality traits. In the startup entrepreneurial context, reflection refers to objectively analysing failures, learning from them and moving forward. Setbacks do not deter leaders and entrepreneurs who possess this trait; instead, they view setbacks as valuable learning opportunities. They are willing to examine their performance, seek feedback and adjust accordingly. Reflection also encompasses resilience, because successful entrepreneurs must bounce back quickly from failures and keep pushing forward.

- *Trust:* There are two elements to trust: self-trust and building trust with others. Self-trust involves having confidence in one's abilities, judgment and decision-making skills. Entrepreneurs who trust themselves are more likely to take calculated risks, make bold choices and lead with conviction. Building trust with others, such as team members, investors and customers, is also crucial for entrepreneurial and leadership success at the startup stage. Trustworthy entrepreneurs are perceived as reliable, honest and dependable, which helps them establish strong relationships and attract support from others.

Entrepreneurship and age

During my conversation with Megan, I asked if the professional experience of an entrepreneur was a metric in their assessment. She revealed that in 2022 there was an increased focus on professional experience and background, and the age of entrepreneurs being captured in the admissions process. Megan shared that entrepreneurs with corporate experience learn the importance of trust, security, communication and emotional control. Beyond these four traits, however, the critical skill from professional experience is learning the value of teamwork and the benefits of interacting with others. This, she explained, is a vital skill and an important trait for entrepreneurs to apply in the startup stage.

An entrepreneur's age is often a topic of discussion in the innovation ecosystem. While age isn't a lead indicator of an entrepreneur's success and no longer a specific metric measured, the Founder

Institute research indicates a correlation between the personality traits mentioned and the age of 34 – the average age of entrepreneurs who completed their program. This defies the myth of the successful entrepreneur being the stereotypical male university dropout in their late teens or early 20s.

I wanted to know if other research identified any correlation between age and entrepreneurial success. A study published by *Harvard Business Review* in 2018 revealed that the average age of entrepreneurs in the US is 45.[4] Interestingly, the study's authors stated:

> Evidence points to entrepreneurial performance rising sharply with age before cresting in the late fifties. Therefore, if you were faced with two entrepreneurs and knew nothing about them besides their age, you would do better, on average, betting on the older one.

So, how does this explain the outliers such as Steve Jobs (Apple) or Jeff Bezos (Amazon) – both in their 20s when they founded their businesses? As the authors of the Harvard research study explained,

> The growth rates of their businesses from the point of view of market capitalisation peaked when these founders were middle-aged. For example, Steve Jobs and Apple introduced the company's most profitable innovation, the iPhone, when he was 52. Jeff Bezos and Amazon have moved far beyond selling books online, and Amazon's future market cap growth rate was highest when Bezos was 45.

Interestingly, the Harvard researchers concluded that while many factors help explain why some entrepreneurs are more successful than others, the concrete matter of work experience plays a critical role. The study reported that 'relative to founders with no relevant experience, those with at least three years of prior work experience in the same narrow industry were more likely to launch a highly successful startup.'[5]

A joint study by the University of Tasmania and the University of Sunshine Coast in Australia in 2021 also confirmed similar findings, revealing that 50 is the average age of entrepreneurs in Australia. The authors of the study stated that 'overall, older age is associated with higher levels of entrepreneurial success ... due to three key advantages: human capital, social capital and financial capital'. The study further suggested that 'mature-aged entrepreneurship is growing faster than it is among any other age group in Australia'.[6]

Just as I have noted outliers in the United States, there are also exceptions in the Australian market – for example, Melanie Perkins (Canva), Nick Molnar (Afterpay), Mike Cannon-Brookes and Scott Farquhar (co-founders, Atlassian). Each of these founders was in their 20s when they established their business. While it is generally acknowledged that entrepreneurs are less risk-averse at this age because they have less to lose with fewer financial obligations, if the Harvard and Australian research is correct, these founders are yet to reach their peak.

DIGIVIZER: A GLOBAL POWERHOUSE

Digivizer is one of Australia's leading digital marketing analytics technology and activations companies, with a mission to help any business get the greatest return on their investment in digital marketing.

With more than 40 staff across three continents, its data-driven platform and services have helped businesses of all shapes and sizes create better customer experiences by knowing more about what people want and care about.

I met with Emma Lo Russo, co-founder and CEO of Digivizer, to understand how the skills she developed during her corporate career have assisted her as she transitioned to starting her current business.

Emma acknowledges that her previous experience working for a technology multinational has played a major part in her success. She credits her extensive corporate career for allowing her to make the right decisions at pivotal times as she's been building Digivizer. Emma explains that her existing networks, global leadership expertise, ability to identify and respond swiftly to risks and opportunities, and her ability to create a cohesive culture have all been critical to the success of Digivizer.

With her international corporate experience across Asia–Pacific, when starting Digivizer, she had no fear of building it as a global business from day one. However, during our discussion, I couldn't help but ask why social marketing was so important to her. She shared that she has always been passionate about supporting business owners, and knew that social marketing was becoming a critical tool. Emma combined her passion and experience to start Digivizer and is now expanding to support more businesses globally to understand their customers using real-time analysis and insights.

Prior to speaking with Emma, I had heard about Digivizer's fast growth in Asia–Pacific and was curious about what triggered this. Emma explained that partnerships had always been at the heart of Digivizer and, with this focus, she secured a strategic partnership with a major multinational corporation in Singapore. This required Emma and her team to open an office to support 14 Asian countries within 30 days. Emma reveals, 'We had very little time, but I had a great team in Australia, so I put my trust in them and sent my best two leaders to Singapore,' said Emma. 'We were determined and bloody-minded when it came to succeeding. This was our chance; we had done our due diligence in Singapore, so we understood the market. We knew that trust, resilience, and communication were crucial, and we didn't miss a project milestone. We look back now on what we achieved and don't know how we did it!'

In sharing her reflections on her journey to expand Digivizer across the globe, it's obvious from our conversation that Emma knows how to recruit great people, all honed from her corporate experience. She looks for smart, talented individuals, with a growth mindset. Emma also recruits those with an action-focused bias, not strategic.

As I wrapped up our conversation, Emma reinforced one of the most valuable skills for a leader of a growth company – to let go of control and trust the team to deliver their individual goals and company objectives.

The transition skillset

As discussed with the Business Growth Lifecycle in chapter 3, transitioning a business through each lifecycle phase requires different leadership skills. A startup leader, for example, must give clear instructions to their teams to direct them on the way forward, earning them the title of 'director'. As the business moves to the scaleup stage and perhaps starts to consider growing globally, its leader must become more of a delegator, recognising they can't deliver all the business outcomes alone.

As also discussed in chapter 3, as the business moves to the growth stages, its core processes need to be repeatable and predictable – and they need to stay that way throughout the process of decentralising the sales, customer support and brand functions to expand successfully. (See chapter 7 for more detail on how repeatability, predictability and probability combine in the Process Scalability Formula.)

The leader's role at this growth stage is to create a responsive and adaptable culture to support the growth of the business, requiring balanced leadership of collaboration and being open to ideas from others. Rather than individual focus, leaders need to create a culture of inclusiveness, develop strong listening skills and high empathy, and foster and act on input from their teams. Leaders must continue to be agile, delivering innovative products and services during significant growth.

As mentioned, the Founder Institute research identified fluid intelligence as being a trait of successful entrepreneurs. I was curious to understand if this trait can be learned by leaders as their business transitions through the business lifecycle. In short, fluid intelligence fosters a business leader's ability to think and act quickly and solve problems relatively easily. Leaders with high fluid intelligence (hi-fluIQ) are better at analogical, analytical, conceptual, innovative, strategic and focused thinking than those with average or low fluid intelligence. These are the characteristics successful entrepreneurs are likely to possess – and are a necessary capacity for a leader of any size of organisation in a fast-paced and dynamic environ-ment. I was curious to understand if leaders of growth and mature companies with low fluid intelligence can acquire hi-fluIQ. To answer this, I turned to cognitive scientist Phillip Campbell, CEO of enigmaFIT.

THE GLOBAL SUCCESSES OF ENIGMAFIT

Phillip Campbell is dedicated to unlocking the brain's power to rapidly improve executives' leadership capabilities and enhance entre-preneurs' ability to accelerate the growth of their businesses.

During our conversation, Phillip explained that for leaders in today's increasingly complex business environment, understanding how to apply new knowledge can be difficult. He added that today's leaders, from global companies to small scaleups, must optimise their ability to 'learn to learn' and apply it to new and complex business challenges.

According to Phillip, the way to improve fluid thinking is to engage and develop the right side of the brain (which is where creative think-ing, rather than pure logic, comes from) and develop subconscious habits that create the conditions for fluid thinking to take place. This capacity for innovative thinking both requires and enables a balanced brain. This is the state that optimises the application of knowledge.

Phillip also shared that leaders at all stages of the business lifecycle can improve fluid thinking – from experimenters to ambassadors. As a result of his work, leaders found that developing the capac-ity to access the right side of their brain to exercise fluid thinking was a game-changer. It exponentially increased their adaptability, flexibility, agility and capacity to pivot in new, novel and complex situations.

Another thing to be aware of is that fluid thinking naturally peaks in young adulthood and decreases as the brain ages. But as a client of Phillip's said humorously, 'You can teach an old dog new tricks'.

The scaleup – moving to a growth business leader

Throughout this chapter, I have focused on early-stage companies, from startup to scaleup. While the skillset entrepreneurs and leaders require at these early stages is challenging, the transitional skillset required by a leader moving into the growth phase is complex. Leading a growth company takes unique capabilities, experience and courage and, as we saw in our case study for OFX, the personal desire to work for a global company.

I was interested to learn about the leadership competencies for a complex growth company and spoke with a client – Neil Verdal-Austin, CEO of SomnoMed. Neil has an intriguing story of combining personal growth, professional development and advancement. Neil was CFO of SomnoMed for eight years and was promoted in 2017 to CEO, a position he currently holds. Neil experienced the challenges and risks of launching internationally from different leadership positions and commercial outlooks.

SOMNOMED AND THE MODERN LEADER

SomnoMed treats sleep-related breathing disorders, including obstructive sleep apnoea and bruxism. It's the world's leading oral appliance for sleep apnoea treatment, operating in 28 countries, including the United States, Australia, Sweden, Germany, Spain and Portugal.

During our conversation, Neil shared two principles that underpin his leadership approach as he builds a successful decentralised global business.

He first revealed the importance of authenticity and being self-aware of the impact he has on his staff, clients and stakeholders. Neil explained that self-awareness starts with self-reflection – knowing his limitations and ensuring he includes others for their advice and feedback. Neil further explained that he always tries to be open and transparent, so he is honest about what is happening with his team when things are not going well and seeks their contribution. For Neil, authenticity is having the courage to remain true to who he is, regardless of the role, and this is a cornerstone of his leadership style.

The second principle Neil shared is ethical decision-making. As the CEO of a global business in the complex field of the medical device industry, an assumption would be that ethics is at the core of the business. Certainly, that is the case for SomnoMed; however, Neil goes further. He displays strong empathy and feels the weight of responsibility as he makes decisions for his clients, staff and shareholders. He is driven by his value of 'doing the right thing' and recognises the importance of transparency and accountability in his decisions.

Neil has successfully transitioned from a highly specialised role as CFO at a scaleup to the role of CEO and has developed (and continues to learn) the skills of a successful and respected leader of a growth company.

***

This chapter has highlighted that defining the leading characteristics of an entrepreneur is challenging. Just as success is defined differently by each of us, so too are the motivations for starting a business and going on to lead its growth and global expansion. While no one formula exists for success, we know from research that our brains can learn to adapt, and this, combined with using our hearts, can be a powerful combination. Whatever formula we use to assess a leader's potential, we know that a leader who does not have the self-awareness to adapt to the company's changing demands will almost certainly fail.

Top 5 insights from this chapter

1. There is no precise formula to gauge the likelihood of success of would-be entrepreneurs, but there are clues you can be guided by.

2. Leaders must improve their 'fluid thinking'. This means the ability to think and act quickly to seize opportunities and solve problems in a fast-paced and dynamic environment.

3. Studies indicate that entrepreneurs are likely to reach their peak performance between 45 and 50 years of age.

4. Previous domain and management expertise in a specific industry can contribute to a founder's success.

5. Trust, integrity, honesty and holding firm to one's ethical position are essential attributes for leaders.

Self-reflection: What characteristics do you display as an entrepreneur and as a business leader? Are there any areas for reflection and professional development to help you lead your business?

CHAPTER 5

GOVERNANCE STRUCTURES AS YOUR BUSINESS GROWS

Be courageous, but not foolhardy.
Maya Angelou

Few of us knew as a child what we wanted to be when we grew up – a doctor, an artist, a farmer? But we all have one thing in common. We all sought advice from those we trust and whose opinions we value.

Just as you have likely benefitted from sage advice through various stages of life, so too can your business. As I outlined in chapter 3, the typical business lifecycle includes five interconnected phases. Each step of the business cycle represents new challenges for you as the leader. From the introduction of an idea to maturity, each phase requires a contingent leadership style that quickly adapts to the requirements of the situation at hand.

Throughout each phase, your business's success depends on your leadership skills to manoeuvre it in the right direction. While a product or service that resonates with its target market is critical, your ability to implement the business strategy with agility, focus and clear communication is the ultimate driving force to success.

So, what support is available to you as your startup progresses across the business lifecycle? How do you and your team – with limited budgets – gain access to experts and advisors who have already trodden the notoriously difficult startup pathway? And when do you need to formalise these processes? When does good governance become imperative to running your business successfully?

Business Growth Lifecycle and governance

I speak to many new business founders with high-level expertise in a specific function – from marketing to engineering, finance and more. Conversely, there is little experience or knowledge across the other vital functions of building a business.

For founders at the prototype stage of the business cycle, support is available from mentors with considerable general management experience. (Refer to chapter 3 for a rundown of the Business Growth Lifecycle stages.) The second stage (startup) involves transitioning the leadership and governance style from a mentor-based approach to establishing an advisory committee (sometimes called an advisory board or advisory council). This is especially advantageous when external capital has been injected into the business. Advisory committees consist of individuals who may already be part of the organisation but often have no (or negligible) fiduciary duties binding them to the company.

This continues until the next stage (the scaleup stage), where the business may be looking to expand globally. At this stage, a governance board is established generally for two reasons. First, industry regulators require formal governance oversight. Second, the scaleup has successfully raised capital, and investors require the implementation of formal governance processes. The governance board has fiduciary responsibilities and accountability for setting the business's strategic direction, while management's role is to operationalise and implement the strategy.

In the remainder of this chapter, I outline these three defining external support mechanisms – leadership through mentors, advisory committees and governance boards – and how you should look to apply them to your business as it grows.

Leadership through mentors

No-one is successful in isolation. Even the most distinguished names in business have a team of supporters who have helped them keep their dreams alive. Many have had trusted mentors under their umbrella who have helped them stay on track and steer their businesses through the most crucial moments. Indeed, a 2004 meta-analysis of academic studies suggested that individuals with mentors experience better career outcomes than those lacking mentorship.[1]

Mentors possess relevant experience in specific disciplines that they impart to mentees. The role of a good mentor is to listen to challenges, share their experience, and work with the entrepreneur to develop an action plan to address the challenges they are (or anticipate) experiencing. A great mentor will then constructively hold the entrepreneur to account for taking the actions that have been agreed to.

Adam Grant, a professor at the Wharton School of the University of Pennsylvania specialising in organisational psychology, summed it up best when he shared the following difference between good and great mentors:

> Good mentors share lessons from their experience. Great mentors help you crystallize lessons from your experience. Good mentors give helpful answers. Great mentors help you ask better questions. Good mentors walk you through their path. Great mentors help you identify your path.

The mentor–mentee engagement is often not time-bound – and this is one of the differences between working with a mentor and a coach. Meetings with mentors can be arranged when the mentee requires advice or support as challenges arise. While coaches are trained to ask questions, explore and then encourage the mentee to develop the answers, mentors ask questions to understand the issue at hand, share their experience of a similar situation and jointly develop a solution. In my experience, mentoring is more directive and instructional than coaching, and therefore it is worthwhile considering the type of support you specifically require.

One of the great benefits of having a mentor is that the partnership can last for many years, and great mentor–mentee relationships mean you can dive in or out as needs demand. In my work today, I continue to work with mentors whom I first connected with a decade ago while working in corporate roles. These individuals continue to impart sage advice, drawing on their experience and knowledge of my career trajectory, goals and values. They know me exceptionally well and can signpost my strengths and areas for improvement. My mentors genuinely want me to succeed.

How can mentors help your business grow globally?

Seeking mentors internationally can help you reach markets in other parts of the world by connecting with their networks, which, as discussed, is vital for early-stage businesses. Also, having an experienced mentor can significantly lessen your risk exposure by having a confidant to offer a reliable and trusted second opinion – one that could mean the difference between success and failure. Overall, mentors are essential to your global growth agenda and bring abundant wisdom and experience of learning from their mistakes and successes. They offer emotional support and can help you to apply the relevant learnings to avoid going down paths that may pose risks or do not align with your goals.

The mentor–mentee relationship

The following sections outline my seven strategies for a productive mentor–mentee relationship.

Set expectations in advance

Setting ground rules before embarking on a mentorship engagement is critical. Agreeing early on details such as how often you'll meet and establishing your goals encourages both sides to stick to the commitment and helps ensure that the relationship continues to provide value.

At the beginning of this section, I mentioned the benefits of building rapport. This rapport should be based on mutual respect – a meaningful relationship between mentee and mentor – and an important element of this is discussing how either side can opt-out if the relationship is not productive.

Remember, it's a two-way street

The mentee isn't the only one who benefits from a mentoring relationship. Mentors also have much to gain, including a new perspective on business challenges and the opportunity to learn about emerging industry trends. However, the overall benefit for mentors is the sense of satisfaction in helping someone else grow, giving hope to entrepreneurs' aspirations, and providing guidance to achieve this.

Be prepared for each session

Since the mentor is usually the more experienced leader of the two, they are sometimes expected to take the lead during meetings. However, while the mentor is responsible for guiding the discussion and encouraging the mentee to work through their challenges, as a mentee you should come prepared with specific questions or topics to discuss and be accountable for taking agreed actions.

Respect each other's time

This should go without saying but respecting one another's time will help ensure the relationship stays positive and focused. As with any professional relationship, don't miss meetings, arrive late or overstay your welcome.

Be honest

I mentor founders worldwide, and all are nervous at the beginning of our sessions. So, during our first call, I share my journey, including my vulnerabilities, and then listen to their situation. After that, it doesn't take too long for founders to realise they can relax into the conversation, recognising that my motivation is to help them succeed.

What's important as a mentor is to recognise that in the first interaction, the founder is in a panicked state of mind. They are often frustrated with overdue tasks and having too many demands from their teams. As mentor, I work with the founder to break down their tasks into simple actions, setting priorities and realistic deadlines. We then prepare for the next mentoring session.

As the mentee, be honest with your mentor. Share your challenges, issues and frustrations so you can work productively with them and bring a sense of order and prioritisation to your work.

Be a good listener

Mentors must practise active listening during mentoring sessions to understand their mentees' aspirations, challenges and goals. This understanding allows mentors to tailor their guidance and support to address the specific needs of their mentees, making the mentorship more meaningful and impactful. Each mentee's journey is unique, and active listening allows mentors to offer advice that aligns with the mentee's specific context and circumstances.

In my experience, when mentees feel heard, they gain confidence in their abilities and decisions. Active listening, therefore, validates their thoughts and feelings, empowering them to take ownership of their learning and development. This empowerment contributes to their growth and self-belief, contributing to a positive experience, making the mentorship journey enriching for both parties involved.

When mentees feel genuinely heard and understood, they are more likely to trust their mentors, which is the next essential component of the partnership.

It's all about trust

Unsurprisingly, trust rears its head here because it is core to any successful mentor–mentee relationship. Trust is crucial in the relationship because it creates a safe environment for mentees to share their thoughts, concerns and vulnerabilities. This, in turn, leads to a more open and honest dialogue, enabling the mentor to provide more relevant and personalised advice. The bottom line is that the relationship between mentor and mentee requires a high level of trust, given that sensitive and confidential information is regularly shared.

As a mentee, I have been at the end of the poisonous chalice when a long-term mentor broke my trust. I have heard of other horrid stories where the mentor has shared confidential details or expressed opinions to third parties in public conversations. Both parties are responsible for respecting and trusting each other that what is shared remains confidential.

A solid mentoring relationship is about building rapport, staying focused on your goals, acting with integrity, and channelling a growth mindset that allows for self-directed problem-solving in a trusting and safe environment.

Leadership through counsel: Advisory committees

Leadership through counsel provided by advisory committees (sometimes called an advisory board or advisory council) is the second of the three defining external support mechanisms you, as leader, should apply to your business as it expands. The Australian Institute of Company Directors defines an advisory committee as 'a group of suitably experienced people appointed to give considered advice, recommendations or counsel in connection with a business, corporate or other organisational purposes.'

Advisory committees are typically established once you reach the startup stage, and receive external funding.

Your advisory committee should consist of experienced business professionals responsible for providing counsel and strategic advice regarding complex business problems. Importantly, advisory committee members usually don't have any fiduciary relationship with the business, and the decisions made by the advisory committee are not binding on the organisation. What that means is that you as the leader retain full responsibility for decision-making.

When is an advisory committee required?

There are typically three factors which indicate that an advisory committee is needed:

1. *Before raising capital:* Some investors want visibility about who is advising the business. They will want to assess whether these people are industry experts and respected advisors. Advisory committee members need credibility in their expertise and a deep network across the industry sector.

2. *Leader skills gap:* Effective leaders recognise their strengths and weaknesses in running a business. With this knowledge they can then identify their skill gaps and where they require additional support and advice from specialists. Therefore, you must allocate time to assess your own knowledge, skills and competencies, and identify critical gaps to secure the most appropriate group of advisors for your business. With this assessment, you then have a structured process to identify independent professionals to potentially fill your identified gaps.

3. *Project advisory boards:* During the growth stage of the business lifecycle, companies face specific challenges and require specialist expertise to advance decision-making. According to Australia's Advisory Board Centre, project advisory boards have 'a clearly defined scope and impact measurement allowing for tailored advice'. The most common are created for market testing (35 per cent), new business models (26 per cent) and international markets (24 per cent).[2]

Features of advisory committee members

Look for the following features when considering advisory board members for your business:

*   *Independent advice:* The composition of an advisory committee usually involves individuals outside of the organisation. These experts are independent of the entity and, therefore, can give impartial advice uninfluenced by any aspect of the business on

blind spots and opportunities. When you're looking to expand globally, independent advice is even more valuable, with insights and experiences of local knowledge and networks available, along with potential impacts on your business's strategic plans. The exception can be where an investor negotiates terms to be on the advisory board to give them additional management oversight and input into strategic decisions.

- *Specialist expertise:* Advisory committee members are appointed based on their skills, experience and specialisation (for example, finance, legal, industry, global markets). Ideally, they align with – and actively contribute to – the strategic goals of your business.

- *Strategic input:* The expertise and vast experience of advisory committee members in their industry position them as the foremost authority in their discipline. They possess knowledge of the highest level that can considerably improve your business's strategic management processes.

- *Access to partners/prospects/investors:* Advisory committee members usually have an extensive business network and are often willing to make introductions. Their connections are likely to include individuals and organisations with mutual interests.

Using your advisory committee effectively

Advisory board meetings should be a safe, trusting environment where you feel comfortable seeking advice and insights from highly skilled, respected and talented individuals. The most productive advisory committees are those where you, as the business leader, are open to discussion and considering different ideas and ways of approaching challenges. That said, you do not have to take the advice offered; it is up to you to decide what actions will be accepted after considering all the input you have at your disposal.

A common question I receive is whether it's appropriate for the business leader or CEO to contact an advisory committee member outside standard meeting times. It is essential to respect the member's time; however, if there is a specific challenge in the business and the board member has expertise in, contact would be warranted.

Finally, keep in mind that the composition of your advisory committee changes over time. This could be due to several factors – for example, unexpected business growth or a takeover. It is common for board members to change in the event of new business circumstances arising. Also, an annual assessment of your leadership skills and competencies to ensure that gaps in your skills are aligned with the strengths of the advisory board members is paramount, and this could also lead to changes.

Leadership at the summit: Governance boards

Founders must understand industry regulations applying to their business, and ensure processes are established internally to comply with regulations and manage ongoing business risks. Countries can apply significant penalties without a governance structure to manage these processes.

Many organisations have engaged me to work with their founders to educate them on governance, risk management and compliance, and the benefits that can be derived through governance boards, including:

- supporting business growth
- managing business risk – ranging from regulatory adherence to financial and cultural
- addressing critical issues such as ethics, culture and environmental policies.

The subject of 'governance boards' is vast, so I have focused on the basics here (and suggested additional resources business leaders can tap into for further details).

Organisations are exposed to a climate of intense competition and regulation – especially when they look to expand globally. With the business world being more complex than ever, your business will likely encounter multifaceted challenges when you and your team embark on global expansion, requiring you to adhere to entirely new rules and regulations. That's why you need to plan well for your business and establish a governance framework to facilitate your adjustment to new and changing business conditions.

So what is governance? How is it defined? The Governance Institute of Australia, while recognising that one definition of 'governance' is not possible, suggests the following:

> Governance encompasses the system by which an organisation is controlled and operates and the mechanisms by which it, and its people, are held to account. Ethics, risk management, compliance and administration are all elements of governance.[3]

A governance board, also known as the corporate board of directors, is a body of individuals with fiduciary (legal) responsibility for the oversight and strategic planning of the business who are required to act in the best interest of shareholders and the community they serve. They have extensive duties, including (but not limited to) setting the strategic plan, which may include initiatives such as international expansion, the closure or opening of a new division, environmental, sustainability and governance policies, diversity and equality strategies, or mergers and acquisitions. It is also critical to note that company directors are also stewards of an organisation's culture.

Finally, an essential skill for all company directors is to remain removed from the business's daily operations – their role is to set the strategic agenda. Management's role is to implement the agenda and manage the business's day-to-day operations. Unfortunately, this doesn't always happen, with CEOs and business leaders commonly citing micro-management and board member interference as the core reason for their resignation.

When is a governance board required?

Leading and managing a business in a constantly changing and complex world is demanding. Stakeholders, including employees, clients and the broader community, have expectations and sometimes conflicting requirements that must be navigated successfully. In addition, businesses expanding globally can expect to be exposed to intense competition and strict regulatory regimes, and be adversely impacted by global events such as the COVID-19 pandemic. Establishing a formal framework for your business to identify, develop and implement strategies to reflect changing and increasingly complex business conditions while applying governance, risk management and compliance oversight is essential.

Establishing a governance board can give your business access to extensive knowledge from experienced professionals with expertise in financial oversight, capital raising, investment management, risk management and business expansion.

Governance boards for international expansion

Companies expanding globally face multiple challenges. Extending a governance board with in-market, locally based company directors can make navigating local market issues easier. With a strong foundation of governance practices in the headquarter market, such as board meeting agendas, board committee structures and meeting regulatory reporting requirements, you're setting your business up for success.

While each market is different, the following are dominating boardroom discussions across the globe:

- societal and economic risks, including supply chain management
- oversight of the global talent pipeline
- diversity, equality and inclusion
- technological risks, including digital inequality and cyber security
- data privacy laws
- environmental, social and governance (ESG) requirements.

In addition, governance boards are often at the forefront of understanding the impact of new technologies on their businesses.

For example, despite limited regulatory guidelines for generative AI tools such as ChatGPT, boards are developing internal staff policies on when and how these tools can be used. These policies are based on an organisation's risk profile and risk tolerance levels, and focus on implementing controls to address the identified risks.

However, while recruiting a company director in the global market to join the governance board is one option, many organisations take a strategic approach to executing and obtaining the support they require. According to the Advisory Board Centre, 'since 2019, there has been a 52% increase globally in organisations utilising advisory boards as part of their governance structure.'

Here are some examples of how this can work:

- Rather than recruit a new in-market company director to join the governance board, an in-market 'advisory council' consisting of local staff (typically the CEO or Risk Management Executive) and external experts (sometimes titled 'ambassadors') is established. Alternatively, customers or strategic suppliers can also be invited to join the advisory council.

- 'Shadow boards' are created, especially where a highly specialised in-market opportunity exists.

Therefore, you have many options on the governance structure your business can deploy to manage your risk and regulatory obligations across global markets. However, the priority in developing a framework is to understand, prioritise and adhere to local regulatory requirements and then create a governance hierarchy to achieve your business's strategic plan.

Every country has a specific corporate governance framework, associated regulatory bodies, and oversight from specific regulatory and governing organisations. Staying abreast of regulations, licensing and industry laws is essential to avoid scrutiny from regulators. For highly regulated industries in the United States, such as the US financial services industry, a company director or highly experienced risk management executive is critical to establishing an appropriate framework to manage the associated risks and ensure ongoing compliance with local market requirements. Often, organisations expanding into markets that operate in highly regulated industries will recruit an in-market risk management executive first to ensure compliance processes and structures are established before launch.

With the business world becoming more complex than ever, any business will encounter multifaceted challenges when it embarks on global expansion. That's why you need to plan well for your business and establish a governance framework to facilitate your adjustment to the new environment. Whether the governance board is extended to include an in-market company director or an in-market advisory council is established comes down to what is best for shareholders, the financial viability of your business and the community in which it operates.

Leadership plays a vital role in the internationalisation of a business. Despite many obstacles, strong, effective leadership and robust frameworks will help you minimise risks and chart your way to success. As your business grows, you can deploy different approaches to assist in your international expansion. These include mentoring, or establishing an advisory board or a governance board, or it could be a combination of these three. Nevertheless, authority and guidance are critical in any major strategic decision, especially regarding the high-risk strategy of international expansion.

Top 5 insights from this chapter

1. Businesses require different governance counsel and structures at each stage of the business cycle.

2. Business mentors play an essential part in supporting organisations through planned expansion. They impart wisdom across multiple disciplines, from strategic policies to workforce development.

3. Organisations need to create a risk profile to assess risk tolerance levels and controls to identify current and future risks, including tools such as generative artificial intelligence.

4. Understanding the regulatory environment is critical for businesses before expanding globally.

5. Establishing an advisory or governance board is circumstantial. They differ in terms of responsibilities, powers and the support they provide. Hence, their existence is contingent on the specific circumstances for your business, including its stage in the business lifecycle and strategic direction.

Self-reflection: Have you established an effective governance structure to manage risk across your business? How might your needs change as your business grows?

_____

_____

_____

_____

_____

_____

_____

_____

_____

_____

_____

_____

_____

CHAPTER 6

STORYTELLING TECHNIQUES TO SECURE FUNDING

At its core, storytelling is about creating a lasting and positive impression.

Anthony Bastic, CEO AGB Events

The most enduring living culture belongs to Australia's First Nations Peoples, dating back more than 65,000 years. Storytelling has been integral to their culture and traditions, passing tales of the Dreamtime, origin stories and history across generations. Through stories, First Nations Australians connect with their land and ancestors and preserve their culture to inform future generations in an accessible way. Business leaders can learn from the ancient storytelling practices in indigenous cultures worldwide. The main lesson is the importance of – and ability to – take the spoken word and cultivate an emotional connection with the audience by sharing the past and generating interest for the future.

Storytelling in business is increasingly recognised as one of the most powerful tools for leaders to strengthen their brands and communicate their purpose, strategic vision and company values. Leaders are accustomed to telling stories in business through slide decks and podcasts, but storytelling is about so much more than delivery methods.

As seen in chapter 3, funding is one of the four primary elements of the Business Growth Lifecycle. You may question why I am discussing storytelling and pitching and not focusing specifically on raising capital and the various methods of doing this. I believe all funding starts with the ability to tell a compelling, engaging story.

THE POWER OF STORYTELLING

Anthony Bastic, CEO of AGB Events, is one of Australia's leading creative talents and international event designers, and he has brought to life some of the world's most inspiring events. His work will be familiar to many as the designer and creator of the popular international tourist drawcard Vivid Sydney, the annual spectacular light show illuminating Sydney Harbour and its surroundings.

Anthony Bastic is a master storyteller. A distinguishing feature of his craft is the time he spends researching the source of each subject to understand what new perspective or angle he can apply to the project – for example, whether there is a new historical lens. Anthony outlined that the next phase is the most critical: what medium – sound, light or visual arts – he can use to captivate the audience. Anthony aims to capture their curiosity, inspiring them to experience or learn something new.

I was particularly interested in Anthony's perspective on what he considers the most crucial aspect of storytelling. Without hesitation, Anthony explained why the opening line of a story is the most critical, requiring deep consideration. Anthony looks for real meaning in the opening line to intrigue the audience, compelling them to want to see more. A great example of the impact of the opening line can be seen in Anthony's work at the Expo Dubai 2021. Anthony and his team were engaged as creative and technical consultants to develop a visual story for the closing ceremony at Al Wasl Plaza that authentically represented the country, and its people's unique cultural attributes.

Anthony explains how he developed the narrative:

During the research phase, I spoke with many locals. There were fantastic stories of how Dubai developed from a desert nation to economic prosperity. We could have easily created the festival with the traditional 'once upon a time' opening line, but we felt most visitors attending the Expo would be familiar with the story of Dubai. However, during one conversation, a mother shared how proud she was that her son was studying to be an astronaut – an opportunity inconceivable to her father, a pearl diver. It suddenly struck me that this showcased the opportunities and prosperity of Dubai and its citizens perfectly. From this insight, the opening line for the closing ceremony was born: 'From pearl diver to astronaut'.

As Anthony demonstrates, storytelling is about crafting compelling narratives that evoke an emotional response from the audience, making them feel more connected to the event or a company's products and services. At its core, storytelling is about creating a lasting and positive impression.

Persuading through story

What can business leaders do to change how they communicate to achieve the outcomes they desire? And how does this connect with funding options?

To answer these questions, let us turn to the senior editor of *Harvard Business Review*, Bronwyn Fryer, and her 2003 interview with Robert McKee. McKee is one of the world's most respected screenwriting lecturers, and his students have won many international cinematic awards.[1]

McKee was keen to point out that business leaders can harness the power of storytelling to motivate staff by engaging their emotions. In his opinion, the key to their hearts is the story.

McKee argues that storytelling is about persuasion and that almost every business activity revolves around influencing. For example, in the business context, this is influencing your clients to buy your company's products or services. Likewise, your workforce and colleagues must be motivated to support your company's vision, strategic plan or reorganisation. Also, investors must be influenced to believe in your passion and vision for your business before investing – whether those investors are family and friends early in the prototype stage, or are angels, venture capitalists, traditional banks or even the public via shares as you progress further in the business lifecycle.

However, despite knowing the critical importance of storytelling and persuasion, most executives need help communicating why their product or service matters. Instead, they get lost in the normalcy of traditional communication, using tools such as slide decks for visual appeal, or issuing important announcements via emails spammed through corporate communications. Their messages often fall flat even when they communicate through carefully researched channels.

For many leaders, tapping into emotion – the core of persuasion – can be challenging. Research has shown that great storytelling stimulates 'oxytocin', a natural drug the brain releases when we feel emotions such as empathy, compassion and trust. Importantly, oxytocin can be generated regardless of the medium in which the emotion is produced, such as print, digital or social media.[2] Therefore, the challenge for leaders is to tap into their emotional self, and then combine it with a traditional data-intensive delivery method.

Richard Branson says it best when he states, 'Entrepreneurs who cannot tell a story will never be successful'. Persuasion is unifying an idea with an emotion. Telling a compelling story is the only way to achieve this; you share relevant information with the audience and stimulate their emotions and energy.

Pitching

In business, we can define several types of pitching, and each has a suite of benefits and particular challenges. You will transition using these different pitches throughout your entrepreneur and business journey – from pitching to friends and family for funding, to presenting to investors, and even presenting to a bank for a business loan. In the following sections, I detail two conventional pitch strategies that are typically used by leaders.

The elevator pitch

Every business leader has heard of the 'elevator pitch', but let's start with its origins.

Many theories exist on where the 'elevator pitch' originated; however, my favourite hails back to the 19th century, and an entrepreneur called Elisha Otis. Otis was a factory worker who could see the risk outweighing the convenience of the cable-run elevators that could be used to clear debris from higher floors. The problem was that the elevators in question were notoriously dangerous – the hoisting cables could fail, sending the elevators and the people in them plunging to the floor, seriously injuring (or killing) those inside. As a result, the elevators went underutilised. But being an entrepreneur, Otis recognised the problem – and the unique market opportunity it presented.

Otis created a solution to prevent elevators from free-falling by adding safety locks at each floor level. However, fear of death continued to surround elevators, so Otis held a public demonstration in New York City in 1853 to convince a highly sceptical public (and

building managers) that elevators were safe. Standing inside the lifted-up custom-built elevator with safety locks visible so the audience could see his engineering prowess, he ordered the cable cut. Rather than fall to the ground, the elevator

Elisha Otis during his free-fall safety demonstration in 1853[3]

stopped mid-way due to the safety locks doing their job and holding fast. Otis safely exited the elevator to applause. In less than 30 seconds, Otis demonstrated the value of what he was selling – and the idea of the 'elevator pitch' was born. Otis then established the Otis Elevator Company, which now moves over two billion people daily.

In my experience, the elevator pitch is the most challenging for business leaders to master. However, if delivered with brevity, confidence and power, an elevator pitch will produce the desired outcome: to spark curiosity and encourage questions from your audience.

So, how do you create your 30-second elevator pitch? Of course, ample templates are available via the web, but these are not particularly helpful because they don't teach leaders how to apply emotion and theory. So, the following is how I advise entrepreneurs to develop their elevator pitches. I ask them to place themselves in the following scenario:

> The day has finally arrived. After waiting three months, today is the day you're attending a conference to hear your business idol speak in person for the first time. This is your business hero/heroine. You're their number one fan, having read every book and every article, and listened to every podcast they've been on. Whenever you're having a business challenge, you think, *What would [insert their name] do?*
>
> As always, you're not left disappointed after their presentation. It was brilliant. And you can't wait to share their wisdom with your team and followers on social media.
>
> However, before the next speaker arrives at the podium, you need to return to your room on the 10th floor to collect a document for a colleague.
>
> The elevator arrives, and you walk in, pressing #10. Just as the doors close, a hand juts out to open the doors. Guess who walks in? You guessed it – your business idol. And only the two of you are in the elevator. They press floor #7, then turn to you, look at your conference badge, and say with a smile, 'Hi. So, what do you do?'

The lift starts moving from ground floor to the seventh, giving you only 30 seconds. G ... 1 ... 2 ... 3 ... 4 ... 5 ... 6 ... 7.

What do you say?'

I have worked with entrepreneurs to develop their elevator pitches using this method. I have seen how combining facts and emotions leads to curiosity and an invitation to a second meeting.

Imagining your elevator pitch in this way helps you offer facts and capture emotion. How? First, every leader I have met has a 'business idol' they can place into the story. Second, they all attend conferences, so they relate to the idea of an elevator pitch in this situation. Finally, they can immediately imagine feeling overwhelmed when we discuss how it would feel if they shared an elevator with their idol. All of that is easy – the hard work starts when they start articulating their answer to the critical question, 'So, what do you do?'

I encourage you to undertake this exercise to help you develop your elevate pitch – and then to practise this pitch often. This means you're more likely to recall your pitch at that critical moment – because you never know whom you might run into, and where or when.

As an alternative, a colleague recently shared this approach to developing your pitch: practice delivering a concise version of the pitch by lighting a match and ensuring you finish before the flame reaches your fingers – keep trying until you get it right. This gives a sense of urgency to your practice.

The business pitch

A business pitch presents a business concept or idea to potential investors or prospects. It typically outlines a comprehensive overview of your business, its product or service, market analysis, financial projections, and a financing proposal. A business pitch is important because it offers a succinct and effective way to demonstrate your business's potential, understand its customers and the market, and showcase your management team's capability.

To uncover the essential element of converting an unemotional message to a persuasive story, you must get to the core of 'why?'

The central tenet is that by asking 'why?' three times, you can identify your true purpose, which is embedded in the personal reason you started your business. You can describe the problem you experienced that affected you so profoundly and created such a solid internal resolve to fix it that you would spend every waking hour and your last cent to create a solution. Getting clear on this is what it takes for you as leader to understand and effectively communicate your true purpose.

Anyone who's ever had any leadership training will have been encouraged to identify and communicate their purpose. As leader, and at all stages of the business lifecycle, this is an invaluable exercise that will stand you in good stead when it comes to the gentle art of persuasion, essentially through being able to authenticate your (or your company's) story. The value of incorporating this purpose into a business pitch – where investors are looking for proof of your integrity as a prospective partner (beyond the dollars and cents) – is hard to quantify.

I suggest the following format to help tell your story when making a business pitch:

1. *Start with a problem statement:* What is the problem you are solving? This includes a straightforward statement capturing your 'Why?' Explain your purpose and how it motivates you and your team.

2. *Follow with a solution statement:* This statement should explain and demonstrate the need for your product or service and the impact it can have on customers' lives. Where you can, include customer stories.

3. *Offer the solution:* Introduce your products by telling how you reached this point and how your team overcame obstacles to get here. Keep your explanation to a maximum of three bullet points.

4. *Outline the opportunity:* Refer to the total addressable market (TAM), serviceable addressable market (SAM) and share of market (SOM). Include current revenue and projected growth.

5. *Provide competitor analysis and competitive advantage (UVP):* Include industry awards, media mentions and other accolades. (*Tip:* Avoid making general and superlative statements such as 'We are the only company in the world that does this.')

6. *Identify your traction:* Use projected growth plans, current sales and key financials.

7. *Provide your business model:* Keep it simple. If the investor wants another meeting, they will drill further into this. If you're pitching to a prospect, this is where you outline your pricing model.

8. *Run through your team:* Include your leadership team and advisors. *Note:* Investors like to see who is on your advisory committee or governance board, and some investors may require a seat.

9. *Inspire with your vision:* What are your plans? How do you intend to grow and scale your business? Provide a projected financial forecast for the next three to five years. For prospect pitching, share your vision as a partner.

10. *Finish with the ask:* This is different for an investor or prospect. For example, for investors, you ask for the capital you require. End with a clear 'ask' by explaining your business's impact on the world and how an investor or prospect can participate in your journey.

Final thoughts on successful pitching

The elevator pitch and business pitch are highly complex tools for communicating with your audience and potential funders. They require a significant investment of time to perfect. Pitching itself requires a high degree of proficiency from you as the leader, but the following are additional tips to support the process:

- *Engage an expert:* As an entrepreneur, I recognise that I have no expertise in creating engaging presentations. So, once satisfied with my storyboard, I call in an expert with knowledge of the local language and culture to create the final product. Craft your story, edit and finesse it, and then allow a creative to design it in a medium that will capture the attention of your audience.

- *Practise, practise and practise:* Once your pitch is finished, now is the time to practise. BusinessWeek.com columnist Carmine Gallo revealed that Steve Jobs rehearsed the entire presentation for two full days before a presentation in front of product managers. His goal was to make the presentation the perfect embodiment of Apple's message. Having confidence when delivering a presentation is essential for leaders, and the key to this is practice.

- *Know your audience:* I have often found that entrepreneurs pitching to an international audience misunderstand questions or feedback due to language differences. Ensure you listen to your audience's feedback and, before you respond, clarify your understanding.

- *Uncover what investors and prospects won't tell you:* When I listen to pitching from leaders, I am not only seeking compelling content, but also assessing the integrity of the presenter and determining if I have before me an individual representing a business I can invest with.

- *Remember pitching requires grit:* While practice makes perfect, pitching to an investor or prospect can require hundreds of presentations and refusals. Regardless of setbacks, determination and dedication to realising your goal are important qualities for any leader. The following case study will hopefully inspire you to continue sharing your entrepreneurial purpose and ambition to succeed.

THE POWER OF PITCHING

In 1920 Walt Disney was a young illustrator with a portfolio of animations and a head full of dreams. Notwithstanding his enthusiasm and the promise of youth, he was fired from his job at a newspaper because, as his manager explained bluntly, he lacked any form of creativity.

For the next seven years, this young artist struggled, working odd jobs to pay for his living expenses, all the while continuing to chase his dream of becoming a professional animator.

Throughout this time, he continually pitched and presented his portfolio of cartoons to numerous potential stakeholders, including motion picture companies that might invest in his idea. However, despite delivering almost 300 pitches – and being rejected every time – he never gave up or took any rejection to his heart. Instead, he pondered why his presentations weren't securing clients. Every time, he adjusted his pitch and tried again to make it perfect.

In 1928, he finally made a successful presentation to a motion picture company that agreed to use his animations in *Alice in Cartoonland*, a film that would be synced to music. The film eventually became a success and jump-started his career as an aspiring young artist.

Walt Disney showed patience and determination, which eventually led to his success. He transformed his 300 rejections into becoming one of the world's most prestigious and recognised brands today.

This shows how much of an impact a pitch can make.

***

Storytelling is an art, but few truly master the power that it can generate. Leaders can learn from those outside their traditional business networks, such as indigenous communities worldwide, creatives and artists who emotionally and authentically connect to their audience, employees, customers and the broader community. Learning how to communicate profound and sometimes complex ideas, delivering them with creativity to convey a sense of purpose and uniting people with a common goal takes time.

Persuasive storytelling is vastly underutilised in the business landscape. While it takes insight and effort to communicate a powerful story that leaves the audience inspired, leaders who recognise the power of delivering a convincing and impactful presentation position themselves to stand out, especially in the funding environment.

Top 5 insights from this chapter

1. Indigenous peoples around the world have storytelling at the heart of their community as a way to pass down history across generations.

2. Business executives can engage listeners through emotion by looking beyond their traditional factually based presentation style.

3. Your primary role as a leader is to motivate all stakeholders to achieve strategic goals. Storytelling is the most effective way to accomplish this, with research showing that storytelling stimulates 'oxytocin', that natural drug the brain releases when we feel emotions such as empathy, compassion and trust.

4. You must convince your audiences on both an intellectual and emotional level. Statistics and facts tell a key part of the story, but logic will only be successful when it is connected to messages that speak to how people think and feel.

5. Demonstrating that you can be trusted is key in delivering an effective business pitch. Your audience needs to know that you are a secure investment and an experienced and capable business professional.

APPLYING
LEARNINGS
TO YOUR
BUSINESS

Self-reflection: Reflect on a presentation or pitch you recently gave.
How effective were you in tapping into the emotion of the audience?

_____

_____

_____

_____

_____

_____

_____

_____

_____

_____

_____

_____

_____

_____

CHAPTER 7

THE SCALABILITY FORMULA FOR SUCCESS

What would have to be true in order for you to be successful in another market?

Ben Ient, co-founder, Seatfrog

Four co-founders based in Sydney, Australia, established Seatfrog in 2015. Seatfrog is a popular travel app that allows users to bid on empty first-class railway seats. Travellers can view available seats and place a bid to upgrade, and the highest bidder wins the seat. After successfully proving their minimal viable product (MVP) in Australia, the investment scouts at Virgin UK identified Seatfrog's potential and the significant opportunity it presented to improve its customer experience and reduce operational costs. A partnership ensued, and in 2019 Seatfrog moved its operations to the United Kingdom.

As a startup, Seatfrog validated its MVP in Australia by identifying the high volume of unused first-class seats. Its market research identified this trend in aeroplanes initially; however, it pivoted due to a highly engaged opportunity in rail. The app increases revenue for train companies by maximising yield on distressed inventory and reduces operational expenditure for travel companies via a custom dashboard that manages business rules. Seatfrog's partnership with Virgin UK has allowed the company to swiftly establish brand awareness across the UK public and travel companies throughout Europe.

In 2020 Seatfrog was named Virgin UK's Partner of the Year and recognised in the top 30 fastest-growing UK tech scaleups, seeing 1415 per cent rise in yearly revenue growth.

I worked with co-founders Iain Griffin and Ben Ient as a mentor for more than two years. I had an opportunity to speak with Ben about how Seatfrog transformed from a startup to a scaleup, and he shared one simple, profound insight for founders to consider at this stage:

> The question I like to ask myself is, 'What would have to be true' – and in this case, 'What would have to be true for us to go into another market?' For example, it would have to be true that our business could protect its current position, or it would have to be true that customers in that other market are similar enough to the existing ones that we don't have to change the product too dramatically, or it would have to be true that regulations and technology are not so different that we have to change the product so significantly that it creates more overhead than is desirable.

I was curious to understand how the different answers to the question may change the business strategy, and Ben provided further insight:

> If the answer to the question is 'We've saturated the market, achieved maximum market share and can't increase profitability', then we have a few options. First, we could look at new product lines to grow revenue from our existing customer base. Alternatively, this would be an excellent time to consider the previous question in scaling our current offering into a new market or industry. These two answers may require different strategies. What's important is to identify the problem first. Only if scaling is the answer does this become your strategy.

Once Seatfrog decided to expand globally, they followed a classic pathway from a startup to a scaleup, going between two distinct stages of growth in the typical Business Growth Lifecycle (refer to chapter 3). While a startup experiments and validates product-market fit in its origin market, a scaleup shifts the focus to managing the difficult balance between maintaining agility and innovation while implementing process management disciplines across the business to deliver repeatable and predictable process outcomes.

The scaleup's core objective

The common oversight that growth businesses tend to make is assuming that they possess the knowledge and market experience that will translate to success in international markets. My personal experience and observations over many years tell me that this is rarely the case. Conducting in-depth research into current business processes and consulting a local market expert to offer insights and guidance are key to ensuring your business is set up for success – and you don't launch into a new market unprepared and vulnerable to failure.

As the leader eyeing foreign expansion, your first essential step is defining your strategic objective – why you are pursuing expansion. The next is to define the outcome you want to achieve: generally profitable and sustainable growth through market share acquisition. Achieving this requires deep consideration to ensure you have the structure, controls, and metrics established and actively monitored.

As outlined in chapter 3, while a business is in the prototype and startup phase, its processes may be more experimental. However, when a business wants to move into scaleup (and then growth and maturity) phase, this ad-hoc approach to processes is no longer sufficient. Key processes must produce repeatable and predictable outcomes to scale into new markets and achieve sustainable growth.

While founders must consider their specific business model, most businesses' three vital processes are sales, customer experience services (implementation, support and operations), and marketing. Additional core processes fundamental to the scaleup's success may be industry-specific. For example, manufacturers should include production and distribution metrics.

To help businesses with this deep consideration of their processes and whether they are ready for scaleup and expansion, I developed my Process Scalability Formula, where:

$$Scalability = Repeatability + Predictability + Probability$$

It is important to understand as you apply the Process Scalability Formula that while standardisation of processes is important, innovation remains critical. Using feedback and metrics to monitor process outcomes and redefine processes instils a continuous learning culture, which is a core objective of process management.

Repeatability

A repeatable process is a set of actions that can easily be replicated. The business world is constantly changing, and the way to succeed is to have repeatable processes across key operational areas – sales, customer services and marketing – that can be applied to different markets. The goal is to reduce process variation, which is important for a company to expand efficiently. The goal of repeatability for any business is to generate the same process outcomes, no matter how many times a process is performed.

Take Nike, Inc., for example. Established in 1964, Nike went from generating a revenue of USD $900 million in 1988 to USD $17.36 billion in 2021, largely due to its success in applying a repeatable formula. Nike's formula consists of four main elements:[1]

1. Understanding that brand management requires consistent, long-term strategy, combined with understanding how this strategy applies to local markets, economic and cultural shifts.

2. Recognising that athlete partnerships change over time and are subject to their relevance in the markets in which they operate.

3. Award-winning design and use of new materials.

4. Supply chain efficiency. As one of the world's largest footwear and apparel manufacturers, Nike does not own manufacturing

factories, despite footwear and apparel accounting for 96 per cent of its sales.[2] Instead, it outsources manufacturing to third parties, with strict controls and metrics to monitor production processes.

Predictability

Predictability is an important construct in business. Successful business entities invariably incorporate processes that ensure a pathway towards goal-oriented outcomes or key result areas (KRAs). Measuring predictability allows businesses to establish processes with consistency to yield positive results. In this way, a predictable workplace flow increases the likelihood of a quality product and favourable outcome, enhancing the reputation of a product offering with customers. It can also improve efficiency and productivity. For example, a 'Service Promise' refers to what customers can predictably expect from a product, service or business.

Apple Inc. is an excellent example of a business founded on delivering a predictable-quality product seamlessly in each country it operates in worldwide. Purchasing an Apple product comes with a tacit contract between the customer and the company – for example, when purchasing an iPhone. By doing so, the customer knows they are buying a device and service that functions in a predictable way.

Probability

The observation that the probable is what usually happens has been attributed to the classical philosopher Aristotle.

Process probability refers to the likelihood of certain results or outcomes occurring given certain conditions. It then uses statistical analysis to determine the likelihood of outcomes. For example, artificial intelligence (AI) systems such as ChatGPT use log probabilities to calculate the next word based on the likelihood of the word that comes next. This feature allows it to generate contextually coherent and grammatically correct text. For businesses expanding globally, we cannot predict the future, but we can calculate the possibility of an event taking place and develop scenarios to mitigate any risk. But how can the perceived complexity of probability apply to an early-stage scaleup – or any business?

Probability is used by most businesses, regardless of where it is in the business lifecycle. Consider a startup raising capital that casts a wide net with investors to increase the chance of securing investment. Or, a scaleup's sales pipeline where every deal requires a 'probability rating'. As I am working with clients to secure global deals, our conversation always turns to 'What is the probability of winning this deal – 10 per cent, 60 per cent, 90 per cent?' That is then captured in a client relationship management (CRM) system where further analysis is undertaken to project future revenue.

Established global businesses also use probability to create scenario analyses to identify different outcomes of a particular process or event; it is critical for decision-making and risk management. For example, retail, hospitality and travel companies use probability analyses to recommend products or services based on past customer behaviour, forecast customer demand and predict the likelihood of an event. Technology companies employ probability analyses to develop predictive models for everything from fraud detection to supply chain optimisation.

The challenge for businesses expanding globally is navigating other markets that are not yet known. Probability analysis is typically used as a critical tool to assess the probability of success, identify and quantify key risks and develop associated mitigation strategies. Leaders can forecast demand for products and services from historical and market trends, create financial projects by modelling different scenarios and assess the likelihood of meeting financial goals. Ultimately, probability analysis provides decision-makers with a data-driven approach to the risks and rewards of entering a new global market, and helps them assess the effectiveness of their strategies and adjust course as needed to maximise the likelihood of success.

Applying the Process Scalability Formula to global expansion

How do scaleups apply the Process Scalability Formula to their business? In addition to considering your financial metrics and culture, if your business is pursuing global growth, you require a laser-sharp daily focus on three specific processes: sales, customer services and marketing.

Sales

In the following sections, I outline how the Process Scalability Formula elements of repeatability, predictability and probability can be applied to your sales analysis. I also outline some metrics to consider, best practices and common traps.

Repeatability

An effective and repeatable sales process can highly benefit a company's growth and profit margins. Every business has a different sales model depending on the kind of business it is. However, a common feature that every company should aim for is to provide all customers with the same quality of products or services. A company that does not follow a repeatable formula cannot consistently generate the desired sales.

As mentioned before, Nike was making waves as early as 1988. At that time, its main rival was Reebok, which was comparable to Nike Inc. in all aspects – including product line, profitability and brand recognition. In 1989, Reebok launched the 'Rebook Pump' basketball shoe, which was an instant success. However, Reebok then moved from the Greg Norman Collection, which offered golf-inspired apparel, to footwear collaborations with Ralph Lauren and Jay-Z. While Nike, Inc. was focusing on building and maintaining its repeatable processes, Reebok was jumping from one business venture to another. Reebok was bought by Adidas in 2005; however, its previous successes could not be repeated. Reebok was sold to the US-based Authentic Brands Group in 2021.

Predictability

Sales predictability helps to ensure that a set amount of revenue is generated every month, quarter or year. Predictability is determined not only by the number of people working to increase sales, but also by the method they implement. Predictability is based on repetition because it allows you to identify a particular pattern in sales trends. Successful scaleups implement a CRM system to track and manage sales. Today, many CRMs have dashboard reporting embedded, including predictability and a simple menu to select metrics specific to industries.

However, navigating sales forecasting can be challenging as a business expands into a new market. Successful sales forecasting requires thorough market research, strategic planning, adaptability and a keen focus on performance metrics. Setting realistic sales goals often begins with using historical data from similar markets or products to create a baseline, and then estimating the conversion rates at each stage of your sales funnel (for example, leads to prospects to customers) based on industry benchmarks or initial data. Finally, consider market trends, seasonality and marketing efforts that may impact sales growth. Set a time frame for evaluating the success of your market entry, keeping in mind that it may take time to establish a foothold.

Probability

Forecasting and predicting future sales is one of the primary inputs to probability. This is vital for strategic planning and budget setting. Measuring probability allows you as leader to predict revenue and develop best-case and worst-case scenarios. In addition, a sales metric based on probability is an important key result area for individual sales leaders. You can track these areas, and if a salesperson is not achieving their objectives, you can arrange for development with achieving success.

Metrics

You need to establish various sales metrics for your business, and monitor and analyse performance across individual, team and company levels, and products and services in each market. Suggested scaleup sales metrics include:

- win/loss ratio
- probability rating
- average deal size (revenue won)
- total $ sales won
- lifetime value (LTV) of customers
- average revenue per user (ARPU) or account (ARPA)
- average sales cycle length
- market share (sometimes referred to as 'share of wallet')
- profitability.

Best practices

The most effective tool to standardise sales across markets is a CRM. This will help ensure your processes are repeatable and predictable. In my experience, regular, cross-departmental collaboration that includes finance, sales and marketing teams ensures alignment and forward progression.

Each sales leader in every location should have their personal sales dashboard enabled, which rolls into the team results, and, ultimately, the company sales dashboard. I also recommend establishing a sales enablement program to support sales leaders with professional development coaching and ongoing support. From my experience building FD Global Connections and leading business development for clients in the United States, generating sales can be isolating. I have heard repeatedly that sales is the most demanding role in a business, especially across multiple markets. Establishing a sales enablement program helps you encourage and support your sales team, even from a distance.

Finally, establish a reward program to recognise sales leaders throughout the year to help maintain motivation and drive. This is true in every market, but regardless of time zone, make a point to celebrate success and support sales leaders when needed. Leader boards and rewards programs can work well in this regard.

By their very nature, sales leaders are competitive people who enjoy public acknowledgement.

Customer experience

Customer service will make or break a business. This is equally true whether service is delivered physically, such as in a restaurant or bank, or virtually. Studies have found that 68 per cent of customers are willing to pay more for products or services from a brand that offers good customer service.[3] Another study found that 86 per cent of one-time customers turn into long-term customers because of good customer service.[4]

Leaders must be acutely aware that customers in one country may not hold certain aspects in the same importance as in another. Cultural intelligence is essential to understand variations based on different values, beliefs and traditions that may shape people's preferences and behaviours. In addition, leaders must also be sensitive to social and environmental concerns, and economic factors of the target market. This awareness is vital for making informed decisions about product development, marketing strategies and business operations. Ignoring these differences can lead to misunderstandings, market failures and damaged brand reputation, while embracing them can open up opportunities for growth and success.

Repeatability

Repeatability is especially important when it comes to the customer experience. If a customer is buying your product, they expect to see the same quality of implementation and support. I have shared my tips to help ensure repeatability in customer experience as you look to expand into new markets:

- A standard hiring profile for sales representatives (for example, years of experience, and requisite skills).
- A standard onboarding program to familiarise new hires with the company's values and processes preferably available via an intranet.

- A standard toolkit that sales representatives can use. This includes sales pitch documents, sales scripts, demonstration videos, non-disclosure agreements (if required) and contracts in the local language.
- A standard CRM–enabled sales methodology.
- Local language capabilities.
- A standard implementation process and client support process.

Predictability

Customers need to feel that the product or service they receive will be of the same quality every time they interact with your business. This helps them feel confident and relaxed when purchasing your product or service. Building trust in your product or service at each touchpoint of your business gives customers confidence to provide testimonials and referrals. Therefore, consistency also plays a role in predictability.

Positive impact example

McDonald's has more than 40,000 restaurants all around the world. Regardless of location – and even taking into account some local variation in products worldwide – it provides customers with a consistent experience at any given time. Customers know that when they go to a McDonald's, regardless of location, they can expect the same quality of food quickly, with friendly customer service every time. The key to McDonald's success has been its focus on the predictability of its customer service processes and outcomes.

Probability

Probability models can be used to create policies to improve customer service. For example, we know customers don't like waiting in queues. Americans overall spend 37 billion hours every year waiting in lines.[5] Individually, Australians spend 169 hours in queues during the average adult lifetime. This is the equivalent of five months, two weeks and five days.[6]

There are services that customers are willing to wait in line for, such as concert tickets. However, as the waiting time increases, a customer's patience decreases. According to a study, 59 per cent of customers would not wait in line for more than four minutes; 25 per cent would wait for a maximum of two minutes, and 73 per cent of customers would abandon their purchase if they had to wait in line for more than five minutes.[7]

To manage this problem, a business with many customers, such as a post office or bank, can improve its queuing system using queuing theory. This mathematical theory studies the formation, function and malfunction of queues. A queuing model using the probability distribution of the number of customers at any time can help determine the customer service experience they will likely receive. However, these theories manifest in different behaviours in different markets, so leaders need to work to discover and understand these, and tailor their approaches accordingly.

Metrics

Businesses must establish, monitor and analyse customer service metrics that align with their 'customer vision' or 'brand promise'. Customer service metrics to consider for your business include the following:

- implementation success score (ISS)
- customer satisfaction score (CSAT)
- customer retention rate (CRR)
- customer churn
- first response time
- overall resolution rate
- customer effort score (CES)
- net promoter score (NPS).

Best practices

Based on market intelligence and accepted cultural language, scaleups develop a variation of the 'customer mission' or 'customer promise' that aligns with their Key Results Areas (KRAs). They establish measures to monitor the end-to-end customer engagement journey, from contract signing to implementation and ongoing support. Using CRM technology, they develop automatic process flows with associated KRAs, and provide all staff with training, allowing their KRAs to be reported directly from the CRM.

A common phrase is 'if it's not in the CRM, it doesn't exist'. This motivates your staff to update their clients' details regularly, especially when staff incentives are linked to the outputs from the CRM. Performance tracking allows you as leader to quickly pivot where the need for remediation is identified. In addition, successful scaleups empower staff to listen for and attend to customer feedback, whether via formal tracking mechanisms such as client satisfaction surveys, or during events or other work engagements. This matters because your organisation's culture is its strategic edge that feeds into your 'customer promise'.

Marketing

Building a brand in any market is challenging, but marrying consistency at a global level with localised nuances is one of the biggest obstacles businesses face when expanding internationally. Foremost in these challenges is that leaders of scaleups must remember that they are a startup when they launch into a new market. Once again, leaders need to focus their time, budget and effort on developing a marketing strategy encompassing short-term sales performance outcomes and long-term brand recognition. The primary goal is to implement short-term marketing strategies to drive sales across the target market segment and, over the longer term, build an emotional connection with the brand to develop strong recall and loyalty.

Repeatability

Marketing is integral to the success of a business and necessary for businesses to bring their products or services to their potential customers' attention. Repeatable marketing systems include campaigns with tangible metrics:

- advertising campaigns
- remarketing of campaigns
- email or text messages for advertisements or follow-ups.

Predictability

Predictability is a critical marketing tactic and a dynamic strategy focusing on driving measurable, quantifiable outcomes and, ultimately, return on investment.

Marketers use predictive analysis in performance marketing to tap into data about audience behaviour, consumer research history, purchasing history, website analytics and other metrics to help predict the outcomes of marketing tactics. This places business owners in a better position to assess which strategies are more likely to work.[8] This predictive knowledge drives business owners' marketing decisions in real-time, making it easy to adjust and optimise campaigns, and respond to market changes and customer behaviour. Performance marketing can be scaled up or down rapidly to accommodate global expansion.

For example, e-commerce websites such as Amazon use predictive analysis to show personalised recommendations on their landing page. These suggestions are based on the user's previous search history, including items they have been interested in and sellers they have bought from. The suggestions can even consider the time and season of the searches and purchases to display highly targeted recommendations. This predictive analysis – and its tailored suggestions – helps the business increase sales.

In summary, performance marketing's data-driven approach and accountability make it vital for global leaders seeking to maximise marketing budgets and campaign effectiveness to ultimately stay competitive in an ever-evolving digital landscape.

Probability

Predictability alone is not enough to determine how many customers will purchase a product. As I mentioned above, Amazon produces personalised recommendations but, in reality, the probability of a customer buying a product is constantly changing.[9] Therefore, marketers need to know the right audience to reach out to at the right time. This is where probability comes into the equation. The likelihood of customers performing a specific action can be determined in various ways. For example, an online clothing store can use email marketing software to calculate the probability of users clicking on a link or performing a particular action available in the email itself, based on their previous interactions with the store's products or website.

Metrics

Marketing metrics for global expansion are available through several channels, such as:

- email marketing, where metrics could include open rate, number of unsubscribes and spam complaints
- digital marketing, where metrics could include impressions, cost per lead, click-through rate and cost per acquisition
- website marketing, where metrics could include total traffic, bounce rate, conversions and session duration
- video and streaming ads, where metrics could include view count, play rate, sharing and total viewing time
- search engine optimisation (SEO), where metrics could include keyword ranking, organic visibility, referring domains and total clicks
- content marketing, where metrics could include the amount of content shared, content downloads, traffic, conversion rate and sales tracking.

Best practices

James Hurman's concepts of 'existing demand' and 'future demand' create a framework that distinguishes between two types of consumers – those who are actively seeking products or services now and those who may do so in the future. Here's what the two concepts refer to:

- *Existing demand:* This refers to the group of consumers who are currently in the market and ready to make purchases from a specific category, either immediately or in the very near future. These consumers actively seek products or services in that category and are potential current business customers. For example, if you are in the market for a new smartphone and plan to purchase one within the next week, you are part of the existing demand for smartphones.

- *Future demand:* Future demand comprises individuals who are not currently in the market for a particular category but may become potential customers at some point in the future. These consumers do not have immediate purchasing intentions but may develop a need or desire for products or services in that category over time. For example, suppose you currently have a working smartphone, and you don't intend to replace it in the near future. However, when your phone becomes outdated or experiences issues in a year or two, you will become part of the future demand for smartphones.

Understanding and differentiating between these two types of demand is crucial, and businesses need to consider their marketing strategy, product development and forecasting through both lenses. In addition, for leaders expanding globally, identifying future demand segments can guide their businesses in expanding into new markets or niches, positioning themselves to capture emerging demand as it develops.

Branding lessons

Your organisation's brand informs your customers' first impressions of your business. Not investing in comprehensive market research to understand future customers' needs can cause your business to fail. A trap I often see businesses falling into is that once a client persona is established, the business fails to deliver its brand promise. Whether this results from the outright inability to deliver or inconsistency in delivery, living up to the brand promise is key to succeeding in business.

EXAMPLES OF MARKETING SUCCESSES AND LESSONS

Major multinational companies consider the outlined aspects when developing new business strategies and marketing plans. Some are more successful at this than others.

The world's largest accommodation provider, Airbnb, used social media to promote its brand in 2015 by asking the social media community to take a picture or video performing random acts of hospitality for strangers, and post these on their favourite social media site with the hashtag #OneLessStranger. Within three weeks of the campaign launching, more than three million people worldwide had engaged in the campaign. This was successful because the creative campaign Airbnb chose had global resonance and relevance, and tapped into its audience's emotions using values that can be highly connective (that is, hospitality, kindness and gestures of goodwill).

The Global Scalability Audit

A common mistake for scaleups is to assume their business success can simply be duplicated in a foreign market. The assumption is that what works in one country will work in another. This viewpoint is rife with risk. As a leader, you need to approach new markets cautiously, commencing with an independent review or audit across your local business to address the needs of your future target customers.

Organisations commission me to undertake my comprehensive Global Scalability Audit (GSA). I designed the GSA based on more than 20 years' business experience, starting with seven years as a volunteer evaluator for the Australian Business Excellence Awards, as an employee of a startup at Optus Telecommunications and founder of two businesses. Clients use this audit for two primary reasons:

1. to receive an independent, comprehensive report on the strengths and weaknesses of their structure, processes and systems

2. to provide their board, investors and other stakeholders with deep insight into the company's global expansion capability.

I use the GSA to address the following five critical areas to test clients' scalability:

1. strategic alignment
2. business configuration
3. measurement systems
4. operational efficiency
5. culture and team engagement.

Strategic alignment

One challenge all leaders face, whether they belong to a multinational company or a startup, is ensuring that their company is strategically aligned. Although no one rule exists for a successful business, strategic alignment is usually one area thriving companies have achieved.

Strategic alignment means that all elements of your business, including the organisational structure, marketing strategy, culture and use of resources, align with your company's business goals and objectives. In its simplest form, strategic organisational alignment is lining up a business's strategy with its culture.[10] When an organisation is strategically aligned both internally and externally, it has the capability to collect meaningful data on its processes.

Experts stress that the best companies are the best aligned. Across the organisation, strategic alignment is crucial for all businesses, but especially for those experiencing rapid growth. You can test your business's strategic alignment by asking these two questions:

1. How well does your business strategy support the accomplishment of your company's goals?

2. How can your organisation support the achievement of your business strategy?

Business configuration

Business configuration consists of the technical and administrative activities involved in the creation, maintenance and quality control of the scope of work being undertaken.[11] To succeed, you as leader need to be aware of all functions of your business, from your employees to the product or service they are providing to your customers. Ultimately, configuration comes down to the team, the structure and the specific roles to support global expansion. For example, recruiting functional experts in critical roles such as Chief Risk Officer or Chief People Officer are important steps towards global expansion success. (The table at the end of this chapter, which displays the profile of a startup versus a scaleup, details at which phase you identify and recruit experts in crucial functional roles such as Head of Risk or Head of People and Culture as critical steps toward global expansion success.)

Measurement systems

As discussed earlier in this chapter, the Process Scalability Formula involves looking at the three core processes of sales, customer services and marketing. Applying the formula at the scaleup stage places a focus on aligning business activities with the key business objectives. Successful companies use various systems such as scorecards or key result areas (KRAs) to track the success of core business processes, using one or a combination of the following:

- *Process effectiveness:* This system measures how effectively a process delivers the desired output.
- *Process alignment:* This method measures the degree of synchronisation between the business strategy, objectives and performance measures.
- *Process reliability:* This measures the percentage of demands met by a specific process, noting how unexpected the outcome is, or deviation from the business objective.

A common theme I see when undertaking an audit is that processes exist, but the measurement and reporting of results are ad-hoc. To scale successfully, you must have confidence in your business's ability to deliver consistent results repeatedly. This is only achieved if you have full visibility and confidence in process management, including measuring outcomes.

Operational efficiency

Operational efficiency is the relationship between a company's inputs (costs) and outputs (profits). Operating efficiently means using resources such as time and equipment effectively to serve the business with minimal waste. The greater the company's operational efficiency, the more profitable it will be because it allocates its resources to produce the maximum output at the lowest cost. This is one of the critical factors of scaling.

Operational efficiency relates to both back-office and front-office processes. The back office can include manufacturing, production, inventory management and operations. The front office comprises customer support staff and extends to the company website and social media channels.

Culture and team engagement

An organisation's culture is underpinned by the beliefs and values that shape its foundation. Scaleup success requires ongoing recruitment, and developing and maintaining an empowering and motivating organisational culture where employees feel they can do their best work.

Employees learn by observing, and in companies (especially hypergrowth ones) where human capital increases quickly, the company culture can often get lost and be replaced by individual agendas. Therefore, company values must be communicated and integrated into day-to-day behaviours so everyone can observe them.

Consider the following strategies as you look to support a positive and robust organisational culture:

- *Invest in training:* Onboarding employees with workshops covering organisational values is essential for all staff. Investing in employee training in culture-related skills and other in-person training can help increase the team's combined skillset and help the organisation's culture reflect its core values.

- *Recognise employee achievements and performance:* Recognition from leaders is something that all employees desire. You should recognise employee achievements, whether large or small, in person, through an email, or during a team meeting to boost morale and improve performance.

- *Keep lines of communication open:* As a leader you should remain accessible to all employees. For example, conducting weekly or monthly meetings will build a sense of ownership and inclusiveness across teams. In addition, creating opportunities to be available to your teams through events such as open mic sessions or roadshows (virtual or in-person) gives you the best chance of nurturing positive and productive company cultures.

- *Focus on employee wellbeing and support:* A great leader recognises the high level of commitment and investment of time required from employees to successfully scale globally. To recruit and retain the right kind of employees to deliver your global strategy, you need to establish a range of wellbeing programs, professional development initiatives, flexible work environments, and social and community initiatives. A mix of local and global initiatives to cater for individual market nuances also helps ensure a diverse culture is respected and supported.

To expand a business into a new global market takes significant time, effort and funds. The Global Scalability Audit provides you, the leader, your board members and investors with the confidence that the business will expand when it is ready.

As an example of using this audit to your advantage, a business-to-business SaaS client of mine undertook the audit in 2018. The results weren't strong, and my overall recommendation was not to expand into the United States at that time, given the high number of 'red flags'. As one example, the business used an Excel spreadsheet to manage sales and lacked documentation of client implementation processes or metrics. I was gratified that my advice was adopted and contributed to improving processes and outcomes. In 2022, the client contacted me to review their business again, and significant improvements had been made, with the business now successfully expanding into the United States.

A TALE OF TWO SCALEUPS

I include here two examples of scaleups that stand out; one was successful, while the other was not.

A lesson: Essential

Founder of venture capital firm Playground Global and former CEO of Android Inc., Andy Rubin's smartphone startup Essential was founded in 2017. The expectations for its success were high, considering the founder's expertise in software and the availability of USD $330 million in funding. The company was valued at USD $1.2 billion before it sold a single product.[12] Yet it closed on 12 February 2020, stating that it had 'no clear path to deliver to customers' its new promised handset, Gem.

Essential offered a strong value proposition; it planned to introduce a phone to the market that would work with every platform. It was a feat that had not yet been achieved by smartphone giants Apple or Samsung, and yet market expectations were very high because of the strong calibre and respected Essential team, including former Apple, Google and HTC engineers.

When Essential launched its first phone in 2017, its materiality, which consisted of a titanium and ceramic body and edge-to-edge display, wowed the audiences. However, Essential's brand promise was unclear. While the Essential Phone was visually appealing, the marketing information, including competitor differentiation, was ambiguous. Its target market did not understand why it was different, or the value it would truly bring to their lives. Nevertheless, enough curiosity in the product remained for the business to continue.

Essential announced the product's release 30 days after the launch, which was delayed to 40 days, then 50 days. Finally, it was released 80 days after launch. By the time Essential released its phone, many of its potential customers had lost interest because it was then competing with Samsung's Galaxy Note 8 and Apple's iPhone 8. The customers who did purchase the Essential phone were promised delivery within a week, which ended up being even longer. After failing to gain traction after its launch, Essential had to cut its price by USD $200 within two months, bringing it down to USD $500. Another month later, its price came down further to USD $400. Sales for the Essential Phone were estimated to be about 150,000 units.[13]

Many lessons can be derived from Essential's failure, such as its lack of vision, poor business structure, overestimating in-house skills and capabilities, and not delivering on the brand promise at critical junctions. These elements all combined to threaten – and in Essential's case, significantly weaken – the success of a company.

A success story: Pipedrive

Pipedrive is a customer relationship management tool available as a web and mobile application. Founded in a garage in Estonia in 2010, the founders of Pipedrive have managed to scale it rapidly and globally. Today, Pipedrive is used by more than 100,000 customers across 170 countries worldwide, and it has 10 offices across Europe and the United States. With more than 850 employees, USD $30 million in funding, 16 operational languages and multiple currencies, Pipedrive had planned to scale globally from the start.

Why did the founders always want to go global? They knew they were operating in a small market to begin with. They also had a straightforward, globally relevant mission – to help salespeople sell more, regardless of what or where they were selling. With this goal in mind, co-founders Timo Rein, Ragnar Sass and Urmas Purdue focused on developing cloud-based software that was accessible globally via the web. The founders also targeted investors in the United States to fund their project, tapping into its abundance of venture capital opportunities. Rein said, 'The US has more VCs and angels. There are more companies, and the concentration of them makes it a better learning base.'[14]

After securing USD $30 million in funding, the gateway for expansion was open. The next challenge was to scale internationally. Pricing globally is a complex activity requiring a significant amount of careful analysis, and getting it wrong can adversely impact the potential for global expansion. Should you price locally or regionally? Or should you favour a global one-size-fits-all pricing strategy? Rein and his team decided that 'It has to be set somewhere, and then we can gauge it globally from there.' However, he felt that using one universal price would mean the service would be over-priced in some markets and under-priced in others. Pipedrive was able to overcome this by introducing localised payment methods.

Pipedrive employees also played a significant role in the company's success. Rein believes that a solid and compelling 'value fit' for all team members is needed to sustain the pace of growth. This is why Pipedrive has always had a very lengthy recruitment process, concluding with an interview with one of the founders to gauge whether a person is a good fit for the company. 'We look for people who are driven, with exceptionally high standards and don't make excuses. The ideal Pipedrive team member wants to work in a team and refuses to negatively affect the mood of other team members,' said Rein.

How did Pipedrive become a success? First, the founders had a clear vision about expanding globally. They created a productive and functioning team with aligned goals, and considered local factors such as pricing and payment methods when expanding into the foreign markets.

The following table offers a general comparison between the profiles of startups and scaleups. This should be used as a further guide to formulate activities and processes specific to your business and industry.

Startup profile	Scaleup profile
Core objective	
Local product and customer market fit	Process Scalability = Repeatability + Predictability (+ Probability)
Confirm problem worth solving, and TAM, SAM and SOM	Focus on core processes: financial, culture, sales, customer services (implementation, operations), marketing
Define end objective; for example, to build an ongoing business, to IPO or to be acquired	
Leadership role	
Direct the team and focus on selling the initial idea of the business	Build your team, assign responsibility and delegate. Focus on resources to build the systems and structures to achieve sustainable growth.
Pre-seed/seed: Raise round of capital	Series A/B/C capital raising rounds
Team structure	
Inhouse: Founder (sales lead), business leader, product/technical lead, marketing lead, and customer support lead	**Inhouse:** Core team plus functional leads of Finance, People & Culture, Risk & Regulatory
External experts: Lawyers, accountants, mentors	**External experts:** Professional services (lawyer, international tax advisor), global market specialists, mentors, advisory committee, non-executive director, investors
Allocate equity to staff and/or advisors	
Establish local advisory board	Establish expansion boards – advisory boards or governance board

Startup profile	Scaleup profile
Primary tasks	
Validate messaging Validate sales and client service processes Business risk assessment Recruit smart people for key roles	Assess global scalability capability with an audit Market entry strategy and launch roadmap Prioritise scalable workflows – sales, customer services (implementation and operations), marketing Re-structure the team to scale
Metrics	

Your startup metrics will be based on your business model and industry. The following are suggested indicators.
 	
Strategy/roadmap:
  % of milestones achieved
 	
Financials:
  Cash flow (current and projected)
  Product costs/gross margin
 	
Customer:
  Cost per acquisition (CAC)
  Customer churn rate
 	
Sales:
  Conversion rates
	Your scaleup metrics consist of lag (startup) and lead indicators.
	Note: These are a guideline; your metrics will be based on your business model and industry.
	
	Strategy/roadmap:
	  ROI (return on investment)
	
	Financials:
	  Aged receivables and payables
	  Balance sheet, income statements with YOY (year-over-year) comparisons
	  Financial ratios
	
	Customer (onboarding, after-sales service and promoter):
	  Implementation
	  Service/support metrics
	  Net promoter score
	
	Sales (product/service/geography):
	  Win/loss ratio performance
	  Probability forecasts

Startup profile	Scaleup profile
Marketing/branding:	**Marketing/brand:**
Click-through rate (CTR)	Net promoter score
Monthly/annual recurring revenue	ROI
	Risk management:
Risk management:	Regulatory adherence
Top five business risks	Monthly risk assessment
Employees:	**Employees:**
Values adherence	Onboarding
Engagement	Resilience
Wellbeing	Wellbeing
	Trust
Outputs	
Solution design	Vision and strategy
Brand blueprint	Process maps (current state)
Service blueprint	Process models (e.g., future state)
Team charter	Go-to-market strategy
Capital raise blueprint	Distribution strategy
	Production blueprint
	International entity structure

***

At the beginning of this chapter, I introduced Ben Ient, a co-founder of Seatfrog. He gave us an insight into a critical question for businesses to consider as they weigh up the option to expand globally: 'What would have to be true for you to be successful in another market?' Ben offers the final word and provides further explanation. He said, 'The question focuses everybody on validating facts and having an objective criterion to work against. Ultimately, scaling comes down to a question of business strategy.'

Top 5 insights from this chapter

1. The Process Scalability Formula = Repeatability + Predictability + Probability; this is an important concept in the scalability of a business across the three core processes: sales, customer support and marketing.

2. Engage an independent growth market specialist to apply the Global Scalability Audit to assess your business's readiness to expand globally.

3. 'What would have to be true to be successful in another market?' is the first question leaders must ask and respond to with objective, tangible outcomes, rather than personal opinions.

4. Create alignment on KRAs to ensure you can come back to it and paint a picture of the aligned benefits to help prioritise work.

5. Marketing comprises short-term sales orientated with long-term brand focus to build loyalty.

Self-reflection: How would you rate your business against the five critical areas of the Global Scalability Audit?

_____

_____

_____

_____

_____

_____

_____

_____

_____

_____

_____

_____

_____

_____

PART III

FOCUSING ON THE KEY PILLARS FOR GLOBAL GROWTH

This part of the book delves into the fundamental pillars that demand meticulous focus as you and your business embark on global growth. The following chapters focus on three critical areas: identifying your customer using the go-to-market framework, sales and distribution, and developing your global brand. Understanding the intricacies of these pillars and implementing effective strategies is paramount for ensuring a successful expansion into international markets.

The first chapter in this part delves into the crucial aspect of understanding the target audience in different markets. A well-crafted go-to-market strategy enables you to identify your ideal customer profile, effectively reach and engage with them, and tailor your offerings to meet their needs. This chapter unveils strategies and frameworks for conducting market research, segmenting customers, and formulating a practical go-to-market approach that paves the way for successful global growth.

Chapter 9 focuses on a pivotal driver of global expansion. Scaling sales activity across borders poses unique challenges, including navigating diverse distribution channels, establishing strategic partnerships, and adapting sales processes to local market dynamics. Through a comprehensive analysis of successful global sales strategies, this chapter equips you with practical techniques to optimise sales and distribution efforts, expand market reach, and maximise revenue generation.

The final chapter of this part, chapter 10, revolves around developing your brand. Building a solid and consistent brand presence is paramount for establishing trust, loyalty and recognition in international markets. However, creating a global brand that resonates with diverse audiences while staying true to its core values requires careful planning and execution. This chapter delves into the strategies employed by successful international brands, exploring brand positioning, messaging, visual identity, and the cultivation of brand equity across different cultural contexts.

By focusing on these three key pillars – knowing your customer, sales and distribution, and developing your global brand – part III provides you with indispensable insights and actionable strategies to drive global growth. The knowledge gained from studying other businesses' lessons learned and successes enables you to navigate the complexities of international expansion, make informed decisions, and allocate your time and resources effectively throughout the process. This part serves as a guide for you as the leader, empowering you to unlock the potential of global markets and achieve sustainable growth on an international scale.

CHAPTER 8

THE CUSTOMER QUEST: DEVELOPING YOUR GO-TO-MARKET STRATEGY

Whoever understands the customer best wins.

Steli Efti, CEO, Close

The failure rate of companies successfully expanding into a new market is significant, often due to insufficient planning. While the first step is undertaking the Global Scalability Audit on whether your business has the capacity and capability to expand globally, the next step is fully defining your client in the target market. To do this successfully, leaders use the go-to-market (GTM) framework to research and determine their target customers. By adopting this framework, significant time, cost and effort can be saved from a failed market entry.

We rarely hear of companies that have expanded in the United States and failed. This is unfortunate because failure often generates the most important lessons. However, let me introduce you to an Australian company, Casella Wines, which includes 'continuous improvement' as one of its company values and who generously shares their story for others to learn from. Today, Casella Wines is one of Australia's most successful exporting companies to the United States. However, their success was not before a significant lesson on how critical comprehensive planning is, including developing an in-depth GTM strategy.

CASELLA WINES: LESSONS

An Italian immigrant family founded Casella Wines in Australia in 1969. With a history of outstanding success in delivering quality wines with a high-end price point, the company launched under the Carramar Estate brand in the United States. However, in 1999, this first attempt at launching its wines in the US market failed. The company neglected to undertake comprehensive research on potential clients, resulting in no differentiation from its competitors.

Casella Wines' existing strategy had worked exceptionally well in Australia, a market it knew well. However, the company made a common mistake I often observe in scaleups. Leaders believed their formulae for success in their local market could be replicated to achieve the same success in another market. Unfortunately, the team at Casella Wines made assumptions about the US market. They failed to recognise that the market was already saturated with wine brands – the more prominent brands supplied 75 per cent of the wine sold, and more than 1600 value brands competed for the remaining 25 per cent of the wine market.[1]

Casella Wines didn't arrive with an in-depth understanding of the US beverage industry, the wine category and the purchase preferences of its target consumer. While US wine judges were impressed by the complexity, personality and characteristics of Carramar Estate wine and their endorsements were highly valued by wine connoisseurs, these customers represented only 10 per cent of the adults in the US. At the time, however, this 10 per cent accounted for 86 per cent of the total wine sales.[2]

This meant that most of the US target audience were consumers who preferred beer, cocktails and other non-wine beverages.

Casella Wines did not undertake comprehensive research on the market to specifically understand its target clients' drinking preferences and price points. Ultimately, Casella Wines withdrew from the US market with little differentiation from its competitors.

Developing your go-to-market strategy

The GTM framework is used by businesses to introduce their products or services to customers in their new global market. The framework outlines the steps your business needs to take to develop, market, sell and deliver your products or services to your desired market. The benefits I have seen with clients who have invested in creating a GTM are significant, including:

- It defines your ideal customer persona.
- It reduces the time to market for a product or service.
- It decreases the chances of a failed launch into the new market.
- It allows you to identify and use your resources more effectively.
- It requires you to develop a realistic budget.
- It defines your distribution strategy.
- It reveals competitors.
- It helps identify the strengths and weaknesses of your company.
- It helps build brand awareness.
- It provides the roadmap for your business to achieve the overarching strategic objective.

The following sections cover the main components of a GTM strategy, typically for a B2B business but which can be modified for companies across industries and target markets.

Market and customer research

Your first step is conducting primary and secondary research to understand the characteristics, needs and trends of the target market and your customers, as well as competitor insights.

Market research

Market research is essential before launching into any foreign market. As a leader, you first need to focus your research on understanding the target market in macro terms, including GDP metrics, economic outlook, and business and consumer confidence. Understanding key issues within the target industry is also critical, including identifying if the industry in which you operate is growing or contracting and if your sector is a priority for governments. For example, in 2021, the US Federal Government during the Biden Administration signed into law a bipartisan bill of USD $1.2 trillion to invest in the nation's infrastructure, including roads and bridges, electric and water systems, and high-speed internet.[3] This bill represented a significant market opportunity to local and foreign companies within the industry.

Your market research also needs to identify the regulations and licensing requirements that apply to your industry in the foreign market. In chapter 2 I introduced you to Skander Malcolm, managing director of OFX, one of the world's largest online foreign exchange companies offering more than 50 currencies to its one million customers worldwide. OFX operates in a highly regulated industry. I learned from Skander that OFX manages approximately 55 regulators requiring licenses, certifications and audits. To stay abreast of changing regulations and ensure compliance, OFX appoints a compliance leader in each market to proactively identify, monitor and report on key risk measures. In addition, instilling a culture of risk awareness to encourage all employees to identify and report areas of concern is crucial to OFX's success.

As well as understanding the regulatory environment of the target market, leaders need to consider if the target market will meet their businesses financial goals. This is done by assessing the size of the market in the following terms:

- *Total addressable market (TAM):* The total possible revenue for your product or service.
- *Serviceable addressable market (SAM):* The estimated portion of your business's market you can expect to acquire.
- *Serviceable obtainable market (SOM):* How many customers realistically will buy your product or service?
- *Earlyvangelists (EVG):* Those early, critical adopters willing to try your product or service when you first launch.[4]

Your market research must also map the competitive landscape. I regularly hear business leaders say, 'We have no competitors'. Your target clients are either completing the task by some other means – often manually – or you haven't thoroughly researched your competitors. It is rare for an entirely new product or service to be introduced in today's complex world.

As you research the competitive landscape, ask and answer the following questions:

- Is there a demand for your product? How do you know?
- How saturated is the market?
- Are competitors offering what you offer, or do they have a similar offer? If they are, it's essential to identify your unique selling point that will influence customers to buy your product instead of the competitors'. The bottom line is that understanding the exact nature of the demand for your product is essential to your success in the market.

There is another vital element to consider, and one I experienced firsthand with an early client. This B2B software company engaged me to undertake business development in New York City. The software they developed was complex, requiring highly skilled programmers and the continuous injection of capital over a significant time period. Given the high barrier to entry in the industry, obtaining feedback from competitors' clients was critical. I secured a meeting with a colleague who was also a competitor's client. As I reflected on that conversation, I realised what they shared was critical to our success. My colleague was delighted to learn of a new company entering the market. Their existing supplier had majority market share, but had become lax in servicing their existing clients, resulting in declining customer satisfaction. According to my colleague, this company held the view that no other company had the expertise or funds to build a competing product. The lesson is that entering a mature market where your competitors have become complacent can offer advantages.

Customer research

To understand your target market's characteristics, needs, trends and competitor insights, it is essential to conduct primary and secondary research into your customers:

- Primary market research involves gathering feedback from potential customers and can take the form of surveys, interviews, focus groups or observation. This helps identify market potential, customer needs, trends, expectations and buying preferences.

- Secondary market research is a much faster and cost-effective way to gain insights into the target market. It can involve analysing trade journals and reports and using competitor data to understand the target market's size, location and characteristics.

This research aims to determine if your product or service will address an existing problem or create awareness of a desirable feature of your product so that customers will buy it. Both scenarios require extensive research. For the former, you need to identify why customers want a particular product and what they expect to pay. For the latter, you need to create a product or service that people didn't know they needed and create a new market by raising awareness of the benefits of your product.

This profound research to understand your future customer is designed to determine your product market fit, or customer market fit. For example, it will help determine if a need exists for your product or service in the market and, specifically, identify what problem it solves. Unfortunately, many companies don't adequately undertake research. A recent research study by CB Insights of 110 startups revealed that 35 per cent failed because there was no need for their product or service in the market.[5]

With primary and secondary market research complete, you can then segment your customers into groups based on similar features such as age, gender, socioeconomic position, location, education and other factors relevant to your business. This process allows marketers to engage with existing and potential customers more precisely and effectively. You can use these details to create buyer personas for your potential customers (sometimes called a customer persona, audience persona or marketing persona).[6] This persona is a fictional profile based on known facts that depict your target customer. For B2C, it may include a name, age, location, interests, traits, buying patterns and customer problems.

For B2B customers, the selling process can be complex and extensive. Your GTM needs to capture the size of the prospect business and who makes the buying decisions. For example, B2B products usually require six to 10 decision-makers to purchase a product or service, as seen in the following figure. (Professor Philip Kotler referred to this as the 'decision-making unit'.)

an **initiator** who shows initial interest in your product or service

a **user** who uses the product or service

an **influencer** who convinces others that they need the offered product or service

an **approver** who usually belongs to the C-suite and pushes the initiative on a bigger scale

a **gatekeeper** who controls the flow of information to and among the other individuals in the buying centre

a **decision-maker** who makes the final decision about whether to purchase the product or not

a **buyer** who provides the budget

The decision-making unit

Researching the specific needs and other characteristics of clients you expect to buy your product or service mitigates the potential for costly mistakes based on erroneous assumptions when defining your target market.

Distribution channel selection

Identifying the most efficient channel to reach your end clients is one of the areas many leaders struggle with, especially if a network of colleagues across your industry hasn't been established. Common questions at this stage include how are you going to reach your customers? What mediums will you use to sell your product or service? Do your customers prefer to buy via a website, an app or a third-party distributor?

When selecting a distribution channel, you will need to consider not only the medium to use but also the contact your customers prefer. This might include direct selling, a partner-intermediated channel or an indirect sales force.

Direct selling involves approaching potential customers yourself, and is usually used when you have control over the sales process or have a well-developed customer base. However, it can be expensive, and timeliness and availability can be challenging.

A partner-intermediated channel involves working with various partners to reach customers. This can include intermediaries, distribution partners, wholesale partners and system integrators. Working through these partners can allow you to quickly scale in a new market while benefiting from their existing expertise in that geography.

If you opt for an indirect sales force, you will want to identify and recruit qualified sales or growth leaders in the new market. You will need to consider the types of skills needed, the recruiting process, and how to train the sales team. This approach can be more costly and requires more effort, but it allows you more control over your sales staff, which I discuss in the next chapter

Brand positioning

A key consideration is how customers perceive your brand, sometimes termed 'brand positioning'. Professor Philip Kotler defines brand positioning as 'the act of designing the company's offering and image to occupy a distinctive place in the target market's mind.'[7]

To be successful in a new market, a dual strategy of short- and long-term tactics is necessary. The short-term strategy is focused on marketing activity to drive sales performance. The long-term strategy is about building brand awareness by tracking and monitoring performance and, ultimately, building customer loyalty. (See chapter 10 for more on achieving a balance between short- and long-term strategies.) Your GTM is where you test, evaluate and determine how to differentiate and position your brand from competitors.

Engaging customers is critical to positioning your brand, and developing a relationship with them is essential to building loyalty to your business. Factors such as providing personalised customer service, product availability and delivering on promises are critical to building trust.

Once a brand positioning strategy has been formulated and implemented, it is very important to monitor performance. This is best achieved using analytical tools to gain insights into your customers' needs, desires and interests. These can help you create messages tailored to your target market, and monitor and adjust these messages to achieve your strategy.

Pricing strategy

I have found that if leaders typically struggle in one area when developing their GTM it is pricing. Determining the best pricing strategy for the new market, considering local competitive prices, product positioning, price elasticity and cost considerations, is time-consuming and complex. Your pricing needs to be strategically and carefully considered to ensure your business has a competitive advantage and is profitable.

The first step for developing a pricing strategy is to research the new market and its customers. Your buyer persona plays a significant role in setting the price for your product or service. When you understand who is prepared to pay for your product or service, you will have a solid basis for pricing decisions.

When launching into a foreign market, consider the following questions:

- *Which product or service to launch first?* Businesses expanding globally from one market to another typically have strong market traction with marquee clients across several product lines. Growing into a new market with all products requires significant investment and, therefore, selecting which product to launch first – often called the 'beachhead' product – is a critical decision.

- *What is your objective: subscribers or revenue?* If you have a subscription business, is your objective to grow the number of subscribers quickly or is revenue generation the priority? Both require significant investment, so companies in the early expansion stage should select one to pursue with rigour. If you want to grow the number of subscribers, you can offer a 'freemium' model with your marketing campaigns. If your answer is to generate revenue, your business can focus on revenue-generating sales.

- *Does your cash runway allow you to test your pricing model?* To gain traction quickly in a new market, businesses often adopt pilot pricing and, for many leaders, this is the preferred strategy. However, if you choose this strategy, you must establish the accounting process to trigger when the price moves from pilot to standard pricing. Many businesses – from large corporations to smaller scaleups – lose significant revenue because they don't track contract obligations and update prices accordingly.

Communications and promotions marketing plan

Developing a holistic marketing plan that details how your product or service will be promoted and communicated to the target market is the next step in building your GTM. Your marketing should be inextricably linked to your brand identity and positioning. You aim to identify how to reach your target customer, from crucial communication messages to channel selection. This should include outbound marketing tactics, such as advertising, and inbound tactics, such as content marketing and search engine optimisation (SEO). The tactics you deploy should help attract and retain customers in the short and long term.

Leaders often select a marketing or public relations agency in-market to support their expansion efforts. With many agencies and social media platforms available, establishing and managing an agency is critical. When selecting your PR or marketing agency, you should discuss the following:

- whether the local or global agency aligns with your values, vision and objectives
- how your target audience will inform the channels and media you need to engage (agencies will request detailed information on your client persona)
- what the metrics of success will be (which must be agreed on prior to a formal engagement)
- how you, as a leader, can remain involved in the partnership to drive accountability and outcomes.

Suppose you plan to be visible in the media and use the media to drive awareness or corporate reputation. In that case, you must identify a spokesperson as your thought leader to represent the business publicly.

Thought leadership is an effective strategy for an organisation to adopt in a new market. This helps build the company brand and position the leader as an informed, reliable source of current information. Done well, it can affect how your company is perceived and shape its reputation in the market.

However, thought leadership is much broader than presenting at conferences. It also encompasses writing editorials and articles for industry publications or speaking on podcasts, to name just two examples. The most effective thought leadership strategies consider both the channel for communication and the content presented. Developing a thought leadership strategy should be part of your overall communication plan as one of a range of tactics that can be mobilised to connect with customers and audiences in your new market. Here's an example of how this works. Identify four thought leadership themes for 12 months – one per quarter. Then allocate three or four headlines that fall under that theme each quarter. Finally, identify the channels through which each communication will be issued.

This approach will ensure you have a clear plan to execute, and to adapt should other opportunities surface during each quarter, which they inevitably do. Thought leadership, like other communications tactics, benefits from sustained, longer term activities. One article in one magazine is unlikely to make a lasting impact in isolation.

An important consideration for you as a leader is how being a thought leader in your industry will advance your vision and company mission. No right or wrong answer exists here – you must determine if this strategy is right for your business. Often this comes down to the following:

- *The business size:* Large, established companies often adopt a thought leadership position, given that they have the budget and resources to support this approach.

- *The desire of the founder, CEO or another C-suite executive to position themselves as a thought leader:* Not all leaders and executives are confident with placing themselves in this way publicly, and often require media training from an experienced media professional. An alternative here is to engage a 'key opinion leader' who is widely respected, has proven experience, is trusted across their industry, and has a deep network to share your business mission.

Choosing your global expansion leaders

Your GTM is critical research to be completed before expanding into any new market, with the primary objective to identify your future customer. However, in addition, I highly recommend that businesses assess another element within this research that isn't typically associated with the GTM. This element is to review your team to ensure you have the right leaders in the right roles – starting in the board room.

Often, it's assumed that the team you have today to achieve local success will be the same team to lead your expansion – this may or may not be correct. Therefore, assessing the key roles you require to expand – internally and externally, such as recruiting a brand agency in the new market – is critical. Jim Collins states this best in his book *Good to Great*:

> Those who build great brands ensure they have the right people on the bus and the right people in the key seats before they figure out where to drive the bus. They always think first about who and then about what. When facing chaos and uncertainty, and you cannot possibly predict what's coming around the corner, your best 'strategy' is to have a busload of people who can adapt to and perform brilliantly no matter what comes next. Great vision without great people is irrelevant.

During interviews for this book, I was curious how each CEO determined their leadership approach. Skander Malcolm, CEO at OFX, outlined his strategy to recruit locally, selecting executives with extensive experience, knowledge and networks in their market. However, Emma Lo Russo, CEO of Digivizer, adopted a different strategy by transferring two of the business's most senior and trusted executives to Singapore to establish its office and build its brand.

Indeed, no one-size-fits-all approach applies when selecting local teams – but local insights, whether from transferred staff or local talent, are imperative when entering new markets. As a leader, you should review the roles you require to expand into the new market and then appoint people with the skills, knowledge and experience to give your business the best chance of success.

At the beginning of this chapter, I introduced you to Casella Wines and how their first attempt to enter the US resulted in their withdrawal. Now let's look at what they did with the lessons from that first launch attempt.

CASELLA WINES: OUT OF FAILURE COMES SUCCESS

In 2000, the Casella Wines team regrouped. Their first step was to recruit a US industry expert to lead the research, develop their strategy and oversee implementation. They invested in developing their GTM, which included a significant roadshow across the United States to obtain direct feedback from its target market. This research revealed important insights to inform their US market strategy:

- Extensive consumer research revealed that approximately 70 per cent of the population did not drink wine.

- The target market's preference for beer and cocktails, and other non-wine beverages was due to a choice for a slightly sweeter, lighter and fruity taste.

- Drinking wine was considered ritualistic and formal, such as pouring a glass at the right time and in the right way. This required a change of behaviour and level of knowledge of wine.

- The name of the wine needed to resonate immediately with the consumer. 'Carramar Estate' was not easy to recall.

Instead of competing with premium wines in a saturated market of incomparable premium wines in terms of quality and prestige, Casella Wines created a new product category with no competitors. Doing this created a demand for its product and a future for its business. That new wine is called [yellow tail].

So, what set [yellow tail] wines apart from other wines in the market? The founders positioned [yellow tail] to fill the void for those who didn't drink wine because of the taste produced by tannin and acid. Its category differentiators were easy to select and drink, and it had a different taste from all other wines on the market. Although [yellow tail] was slightly more expensive than other budget wines, that price added to its perceived value as a unique brand.

Instead of opting for expensive marketing campaigns, [yellow tail] used simple and vibrant packaging and placed its products in retail stores for all to see.

However, another element was critical with the timing of its launch campaign – the 2000 Sydney Olympics. At this time, the Australian government was investing significantly in the American market to attract visitors to Australia to attend the Olympic Games. Casella Wines leveraged the timing and brand messaging with its classic Australian label featuring an image of a nationally famous animal – the kangaroo.

This highlights how leaders can use domestic assets – such as iconic animals – to appeal to the American market. This can be very effective as a communication strategy because it offers a distinct differentiation tool that works well as brands position themselves for global audiences.

The result was that Carramar Estate sold 1 million cases (12 million bottles) of [yellowtail] in 2003, its first year, easily surpassing its projected sales of 25,000 units.

***

Many critical elements require deep research as you develop your GTM strategy. However, from the lessons highlighted by leaders from the companies I have discussed, we can see that the investment of time and effort in your strategy helps determine whether your business will become one of your industry's most successful global companies.

Top 5 insights from this chapter

1. Entrepreneurs must remember that the same formula of success in one market cannot consistently be replicated to achieve the same when expanding into another market. This applies to everything from your communications and marketing to customer research.

2. A go-to-market (GTM) strategy is a business strategy devised especially for launching a new product or service to a local or foreign market.

3. A strong GTM strategy contains six ingredients: market and customers, offering, brand positioning, pricing, communications and distribution. I also recommend assessing your team – starting with your board – to ensure you have the skills and experience to achieve your growth ambitions.

4. GTM strategies provide many benefits, such as reducing the time to market, improving customer experience and building brand awareness.

5. A GTM strategy does not guarantee success but significantly reduces the chances of a failed launch and the costs associated with failure.

Self-reflection: Are you satisfied that you understand your future clients in the target market? How would you like your brand to be perceived in the target market?

_____

_____

_____

_____

_____

_____

_____

_____

_____

_____

_____

_____

_____

CHAPTER 9

SALES AND DISTRIBUTION STRATEGIES

To build a long-term, successful enterprise, when you don't close a sale, open a relationship.

Patricia Fripp, speaker, speech coach and author

Expanding a business into a new market globally has always been challenging, and the COVID-19 pandemic has forced us to reconsider how to achieve success. Leaders who established their presence in global markets before the pandemic have had to master the art of leading virtually. However, leaders who have launched globally since international borders opened have struggled as they pivot, adapt and seek novel ways by adopting new frameworks and mindsets to build networks and methods to win customers.

The learning curve of business leaders, CEOs and sales executives has expanded exponentially since the world entered various degrees of 'lockdowns' from March 2020. Leaders are tapping into new offshore networks, building trust virtually, managing multiple time zones and mastering virtual protocols for successful calls. They are also dealing with an exponential increase in the competency levels required for desk-based market research to identify and secure clients in their target market.

But what does the future look like? Many opinions have been offered across social media platforms about whether businesses can win sales (or raise capital) virtually. Will the hybrid model combining remote and in-person activity deliver the productivity leaders expect? I am yet to see a definitive answer with convincing arguments on either side of the debate. However, in my experience in representing clients as their business development interim executive, the hybrid model works; ask any professional sales leader if they chaired successful virtual meetings before COVID-19, and the answer is most likely to be 'yes'. What has changed is that the efficiency and effectiveness of organising, preparing and conducting sales calls virtually have improved and evolved into being generally accepted as how business is done. We now have more experience using virtual tools to do business remotely – which can be advantageous and horizon-expanding for leaders who look to expand into new markets. These changes have affected sales and distribution strategies for businesses entering new markets. I discuss these distribution strategies later in this chapter.

First, however, I have observed with clients another change as a result of the pandemic – one that relates to their wellbeing.

Heeding the dangers of the 'fly-in fly-out' model

Before March 2020, a traditional practice for leaders expanding globally was to adopt a 'fly-in fly-out' (FIFO) model as their sales and distribution strategy. Leaders boarding an international long-haul flight every six to eight weeks was considered normal. From Australia, where I am based, that means around a 10-hour flight to Singapore, plus an almost 14-hour flight onto London, a 15-hour flight to the West Coast of the United States, or an over 22-hour flight to New York City.

However, as many frequent travellers will attest, this kind of schedule has the potential to affect your physical and mental health, and adversely impact your family life. For example, a highly respected CEO in my network undertook FIFO for three years. This entailed a 44-hour round trip in flights alone every six weeks, as he travelled between the East Coast of the United States and Australia to launch his business. This unquestionably took its toll – to the point where he needed to step back due to mental health challenges and the realisation that it was time to reconnect with his family. When sharing his story with his network, this CEO warned other founders of the negative impact of the FIFO model. While it was difficult learning about his experience and his struggle to recover his mental and physical health, his bravery in sharing his situation was applauded.

Navigating the mental and physical challenges of travel

As an international corporate executive and now a global CEO, I have earned my share of frequent flyer points and learned to navigate travel's mental and physical challenges. Taking a business abroad takes ambition and drive. In addition to exercising outdoors when you land, eating well and hydrating, the following are some strategies I have adopted to manage these demands:

- *Caring for your physical and mental health must be your priority:* When I first started travelling for clients, I scheduled meetings from the moment I arrived at my hotel. This was detrimental to my health and performance. I now know how jetlag impacts me, so my schedule is aligned to this.

- *Ensure your family is supported while you are travelling:* The ideal situation is if your family can travel with you. However, this isn't always possible so give them a copy of your itinerary and organise video calls and send regular text messages. Depending on the time zone, I schedule at least two video calls per day. I also ensure my family wakes to an email.

- *Arrange for one of your team to have full delegated responsibility while you are travelling:* They become the primary contact for your team and manage issues that arise, freeing you to focus on meetings and networks. A daily call with your delegate should suffice to receive an update and discuss critical issues. Failing to establish a delegate can have devastating consequences – as an example, I had a terrifying incident with a client who tried to manage his Australian HQ team while travelling with me to meet investors and prospects on the East Coast of the United States. Despite my counsel during our trip, he continued to work across both time zones. This ended poorly, requiring medical intervention.

- *Use a travel agent:* Searching and booking flights and accommodation wastes valuable time. Use a travel agent, or if your business has the required travel spend, use a travel management company.

- *Get into a routine:* Since 2014, I have stayed at the same location in Manhattan and flown the same airline. Not only does familiarisation with their services minimise stress, but as a regular traveller, those all-important loyalty benefits add up. I have found that routine allows me to focus on clients.

- *Provide input into your itinerary:* When you're travelling offshore, ensure you have visibility of your itinerary and provide feedback. I recall several occasions during my corporate career when business meetings commenced the day after I arrived in New York City from Australia, after a 22-hour long-haul flight. Meetings or conferences were held for three to five consecutive days, plus client events most evenings. Not surprisingly, my productivity levels were not at my usual standard due to jetlag. I have learnt that after arriving at my destination I need to allow 24 hours before my first meeting to acclimatise to the new time zone.

- *Prepare to return home to your family:* I stay two additional days to finalise tasks from my trip before travelling home. This is important and allows me to be fully present with family when I arrive.

- *Extend for a holiday:* As a frequent business traveller, aligning family schedules so we can enjoy valuable leisure time together is not always possible, but important to prioritise.

Taking advantage of changes post-COVID

Leaders still need to travel to open new markets. There is no substitute for an in-person presence to help cultivate strong networks of potential clients and partners. So, with international borders now open again and more leaders realising the productivity benefits of the virtual space than ever before, what other changes are taking place?

First, I am noticing that leaders focus more on market research before they travel. Leaders are more strategic about the networking groups they join, meetings they organise and conferences they attend. This also helps maximise precious time spent in-market, with a finite number of hours, days and weeks to achieve their trip goals.

Second, I have noticed another trend from several clients. With laser-focused market research complete, they travel with their families to the target market for the maximum period of time their visa allows. During this extended time, they build networks, meet with potential partners and prospects, and recruit distribution partners. Also, they are enjoying the benefits of exploring new locations with their families. The opportunity to build brand awareness of their company combined with new family experiences means these leaders have essentially got the best of both worlds.

This brings me to look more closely at the distribution models these leaders – and you – might consider.

Modern distribution models

Since COVID-19 struck, onshore specialist sales organisations have enhanced their services to support foreign scaleups virtually. As the leader of a scaleup, your choice is plentiful, but selecting the most appropriate distribution model based on your business requirements, budget, offshore experience and alignment with your purpose and values is critical.

When I work with clients on their distribution strategies to enter a new market, we map the options available according to their industry and specific needs. Unless, of course, funds are available to leap straight into recruiting a full-time sales representative, the following pathway is typical for B2B tech companies:

1. inside sales partner
2. interim sales professional
3. full-time sales representative
4. formal partnership.

Inside sales partner

Engaging an 'inside sales' partner offshore is a popular, relatively low-cost first phase to developing a sales pipeline in a target market. Organisations using this approach access sophisticated technology to profile, identify and subsequently make initial contact with target customers. As a result, their leads are credible. Once a prospect is validated via an initial call, the 'warm' leads are transferred to the scaleup to progress the sales process.

According to authors Andris Zoltners, Prabhakant Sinha and Sally Lorimer in the *Harvard Business Review*,

> Inside sales has muscled its way into serving larger customers with complex needs. Also, inside salespeople who once performed only simple tasks (generating leads, getting renewals) are doing more complex steps, including assessing customer needs, crafting solutions, and closing sales.[1]

Many organisations falsely assume that 'inside sales' organisations are the B2B equivalent of 'consumer telemarketing', which is incorrect. The inside sales companies that I refer my clients to are established and offer the following:

- deep industry specialisation
- current, relevant contacts within their networks
- being at the forefront of knowledge of their specific industries – meaning they can offer deep insights into current and new business opportunities
- ability to build custom-designed sales playbooks with clients
- outcomes focused with regular reporting available.

Interim sales professional

The next option for scaleups expanding into new markets is to recruit an in-market interim sales professional (ISP) who acts on behalf of the scaleup part-time. ISPs are not a new phenomenon, but since COVID-19 and border closures, demand has increased. Even with borders open again, recruiting an ISP should be considered a viable option.

ISPs are an innovative, cost-effective choice and are passionate about the industry they specialise in. They have both a deep and broad existing network, often built during their previous experience working in-house at a corporation. They attend conferences as a dedicated representative of the scaleup and can immediately identify prospects and manage the sales cycle, including initial pitches and demos, involving the scaleup as required.

When first engaged, ISPs require training on the products or services available for selling. A critical step, therefore, is ensuring they are 'inducted' appropriately into your business – which includes creating communication channels with key internal stakeholders, and developing custom sales processes, market-specific pitch presentations and video demonstrations. Also, I regularly see a struggle between who owns the prospect – you as the client, or the ISP whose prospect is within their network. My advice is that once an ISP has introduced the prospect to their client (the scaleup), the prospect should then be captured in the client's CRM, which allows ongoing engagement should the ISP relationship end. It is important to acknowledge this before formalising the partnership with the ISP. This leads to the next critical step in partnering with an ISP – monitoring performance. Set goals at the outset of the partnership, and monitor these on a weekly basis.

Essentially, the best partnerships I have observed between a client and an ISP are when the ISP becomes an extension of the sales team. They are integral to your business as they offer local competitor and industry insights, and offer an understanding of cultural nuances and business protocols. They also become a valuable source of market knowledge with local client feedback to inform product development opportunities moving forward.

ISPs are typically engaged on either a monthly retainer, sales commission structure or a combination of both. Interestingly, while I have seen some clients attempt to recruit their ISP for full-time positions, most ISPs prefer the flexibility to work independently. Their goal is to ensure you win contracts and generate revenue so you can recruit a full-time sales representative. They are an ISP for a reason. They don't want a job for life. In a sense, success to them involves making themselves redundant.

Full-time sales representative

The next level involves hiring a full-time sales representative or growth leader offshore. This can be expensive and fraught with risk, so investing time in recruiting the appropriate person with the required industry, network and sales expertise, and ability to work across time zones is critical. Also, since this person is typically the first global recruit for your business, and often the only employee in that market, a high degree of self-motivation and regular communication with the head office is crucial.

As leader, you must ensure your full-time sales representatives fully understand their responsibilities, including their delegation of authority. In other words, what decision-making authority will you offer? This is especially important where different time zones are involved. You want prospects to experience a quick decision-making process and not be restricted by the sales representative's lack of authority. To support your full-time sales representative, consider the following questions when establishing their authority level:

- What authority do they have for pricing decisions?
- Can they promise a prospect a new product feature to win a contract?
- What access to team calendars do they require to book meetings?
- What expenses can they incur, and how much?

Finally, leaders often underestimate the complexity of hiring an employee offshore, where HR compliance, local benefits and payroll tax obligations are necessary. Therefore, I recommend you engage a local third-party HR and payroll provider, especially for the first round of recruitment.

When clients engage me to develop their distribution strategy, I sometimes blend 'inside sales' with traditional 'field sales' (that is, through the use of an ISP). Supporting your ISP with 'warm' validated leads generated from an inside sales organisation can result in considerable success. Making this work requires a significant leadership effort, with coordination, process management and a robust partnership-driven approach.

Formal partnership

The final option to consider as part of a distribution strategy is entering into a partnership. Many companies successfully enter new markets by partnering with an in-market organisation that has an established market presence and strong brand recognition. Identifying the right partner involves significant research, engagement and alignment with company values and objectives. It's also critical that both organisations have a shared appreciation of the strategic challenges they must solve. A common misstep for scaleups is to partner with a large, established brand and then fall victim to becoming a lower priority. However, partnering can be highly successful for scaleups when both parties are committed to measuring performance objectives and holding regular meetings to review progress.

The following two case studies demonstrate how to create and maintain a successful business partnership.

SEATFROG AND VIRGIN UK PARTNERSHIP

I introduced you to Ben Ient, co-founder at Seatfrog, a travel app that allows travellers to bid on empty first-class railway seats, in chapter 7. Established in Australia, Seatfrog moved its entire team to the United Kingdom after being unexpectedly contacted by Virgin UK.

Their partnership with Virgin UK allowed the team to swiftly establish brand awareness across the UK public and with travel companies throughout Europe. So how does a small Australian startup launched in 2015 secure a partnership in 2019 with one of the most recognised brands in the world today? And how did they come to be named Virgin UK's 'Partner of the Year' in 2020?

I sought answers to these questions during my conversation with Ben, who led product design at Seatfrog. Ben shared that despite being based in Sydney, Virgin UK heard about their travel app, and contacted the Seatfrog team directly.

Following the first call with Virgin UK, the four Seatfrog founders met to discuss their next step. Collectively, they had brand and digital product agency background and extensive experience working with major corporations, which proved to be valuable as they developed their partnership approach. They knew how to run workshops and communicate their research findings and proposed strategies. They understood the value of perception and ensured everything – from the way they dressed to their language and presentation – was aligned with what Virgin would expect from other partners they engage. Their collateral was well-designed and professional. Ben also shared that all interactions with Virgin UK were well prepared for and executed, including circulating the agenda's program and pre-reading 24 hours before meetings and sending follow-up emails within 24 hours of meetings. The Seatfrog team was fully focused on delivering superior services across all touchpoints and engagements.

The professionalism from the Seatfrog team was recognised by Virgin UK, who then introduced Ben to their technical agency to set up details and write the rules. After each workshop, Seatfrog presented the findings back to Virgin UK to ensure they had captured exactly what was required. The feedback from Virgin UK was outstanding – and best said by Ben who shared the following: 'Virgin UK told us this was the best process they had ever been through. They knew we were a startup, so we just had to ensure we gave them confidence that we knew what we were doing.'

I was curious to understand Ben's tips for a successful partnership. This is what he shared:

1. Complete a stakeholder map to ensure you know who they are and their key concerns and motivations.
2. Make sure you fully understand (and clearly articulate) what the product is delivering in relation to the problem you are solving for your partner.
3. Be organised: pre-plan everything and ensure all team members understand their roles.
4. Make it easy for the partner to do their job; provide documentation or support with their agency partners to help them understand what they need to deliver to enable your team to do what they need to do to ensure the partnership is a success.
5. Never take the value of the partnership for granted or think/act as if it was your right to be there.
6. Be clear on the compensation structure of the program.

Seatfrog's partnership with Virgin UK allowed the team to swiftly establish brand awareness across the UK and connect with travel companies throughout Europe. As a result, as I mentioned earlier, Seatfrog was named Virgin UK's 'Partner of the Year' in 2020 and was recognised in the top 30 fastest-growing UK tech scaleups, with 1415 per cent yearly revenue growth (YE 2020 revenue).

Successful partnerships are driven by aligning each company's strategic goals, typically for businesses looking to leverage each other's respective capabilities. However, co-founder of Digivizer, Emma Lo Russo, who I introduced in chapter 4, has a business model that is based on customising partnerships depending on which stage they are at with their business lifecycle.

DIGIVIZER'S UNIQUE APPROACH

Digivizer provides a platform delivering real-time marketing analytics to clients across the globe. Emma's partnership approach is unique and I was keen to learn how she approaches her model of combining commercial requirements with an altruistic philosophy.

What I learnt from Emma was Digivizer's partnership strategy is built around a referral model, and for every referral they generate, her partners help her to scale incrementally – increasing Digivizer's and the partners' user base. Emma further explained that if she negotiates with an organisation to give a partner's members access to the Digivizer platform for three months, for example, this might secure 150 new users. In effect, the model accelerates Digivizer's scale with the multiplier effect.

Emma shared how she combines this commercial focus with her passion to support startups philanthropically. In Emma's words: 'It's also important to me that we support our local startup ecosystem. We believe that digital is the future, and founders know they need to focus on growing their client base through digital platforms but they don't necessarily have the digital knowledge or the budget to do it well. So, we bring them onto our platform to support their growth and offer blogs, podcasts and our Training Academy to assist with building their marketing capability.'

Digivizer has grown significantly through the pandemic and continues to expand as organisations sign up to the platform, recognising that measuring and analysing their digital footprint with an expert partner is a means to scale.

***

The pandemic has forced us all to consider new, innovative ways of doing business – and scaling globally has its unique challenges. However, if it's taught us anything about launching into a new market, it is that we can scale and achieve strategic objectives by combining lessons of virtual leadership with a physical presence. COVID-19 has forced us into offering or leveraging new models for scaling and methods to sell, either directly or via partnerships.

Top 5 insights from this chapter

1. The learning curve of the business leader, CEO and sales executive has expanded exponentially and at lightning speed since March 2020. They are accessing new offshore networking groups and mastering online protocols to build trust virtually.

2. Before the COVID-19 pandemic, a traditional practice for leaders expanding globally was to adopt the 'fly-in fly-out' (FIFO) model. However, a new hybrid model is now emerging, significantly decreasing the impact on founders' physical and mental health and their families.

3. Businesses can adopt several distribution strategies to enter a new market, but these require significant research before determining the appropriate approach.

4. Companies must consider individual business requirements, budget, offshore experience and alignment with their purpose and values when considering their distribution strategy.

5. The partnership model can deliver significant benefits, both commercially and altruistically, and play a pivotal role in amplifying your voice and enabling deeper relationships through existing relationships.

APPLYING
LEARNINGS
TO YOUR
BUSINESS

Self-reflection: Regardless of your chosen distribution strategy, have you established mutually agreed sales incentives, and how regularly are you tracking these?

CHAPTER 10

BUILDING A GLOBAL BRAND

Conceptualising the ideal brand image is one thing, but living it authentically is another. Unless a brand's storytelling aligns with its story-doing, customers will see right through it – and it will never stand up to the scrutiny of a global audience.

April White, CEO, Trust Relations

In the ever-evolving business landscape, where borders blur, markets expand and competition intensifies, how brands communicate in new territories becomes pivotal. Within these uncharted realms, a global brand's true power and potential come to fruition. The impact is profound, extending far beyond mere recognition and profit margins. A robust global brand can transcend cultural, linguistic and geographical boundaries, forging connections that resonate on a profoundly human level. It wields the capacity to shape perceptions, inspire loyalty and influence behaviours while navigating the intricate tapestry of diverse markets. This chapter explores strategies to leave an indelible mark on the world stage.

If showcasing your brand on billboards in Times Square, New York or on the sails of Sydney Opera House during the New Year's Eve celebrations feels unreachable at this stage of your business, consider that the world's 10 most valuable brands[1] once faced the same challenges. Branding ads for Apple, Google, Microsoft, Amazon, McDonald's, Visa, Tencent, Louis Vuitton, MasterCard and Coca-Cola are displayed in iconic locations worldwide. Contributing to the success of these global brands is their ongoing research over an extended time to define and continuously redefine their customers' problems, allocate appropriate budgets to engage their customers in strategic locations authentically, and ultimately gain customer loyalty.

What is branding?

A brand encompasses a business's (or its products') collective perception, reputation and recognition. It represents the unique identity and value proposition that sets a business apart from its competitors. A brand is not just a logo or a name; it encompasses the entire customer experience, including the emotional and psychological associations customers form with the business.

A well-established brand provides the following benefits:

1. *Increased recognition and recall:* A strong brand enhances visibility, making it easier for customers to recognise and remember your business.

2. *Customer loyalty:* A trusted brand creates customer loyalty, leading to repeat business and advocacy.

3. *Competitive advantage:* A well-differentiated brand can help you stand out in a crowded marketplace and attract new customers.

4. *Premium pricing:* Brands with a strong reputation can command premium pricing for their products or services.

5. *Business expansion:* A recognised brand can facilitate geographical expansion and diversification into new markets much more easily.

Few of the top 10 most valuable global brands retain their position; however, those that do share the following attributes;

- *Consistent innovation:* These brands continually introduce innovative products and services that address consumer needs and preferences, keeping them at the forefront of their respective industries. Apple, for example, which I will discuss later in this chapter, is known for innovative products.

- *Strong customer experience:* McDonald's has developed strong brand recognition with its golden arches and consistent customer experience worldwide. Top companies provide consistent customer experiences, products and services while focusing on customer satisfaction in every market they operate in.

- *Brand authenticity:* These brands have established a distinct identity and remained true to their core values over time, creating customer trust and loyalty. In 1854, a young craftsman, Louis Vuitton, established his company, specialising in high-quality, stylish luggage for the discerning traveller. Today, the brand leverages the story of its heritage to connect with wealthy consumers who value exclusivity, craftsmanship and superior materials. While the brand has remained true to its original core values for more than 169 years, it has recognised the importance of developing new policies towards taking action in areas such as sustainability and social responsibility.

- *Marketing for long- and short-term results:* Successful brands understand how to manage the tension between short-term strategies to yield quick results, such as immediate sales boosts, and long-term marketing strategies to build their brand. Research demonstrates that a balanced approach, combining short-term sales activation with long-term brand building, can be more effective in the long run. Further, applying the '60:40' rule suggests that marketing budgets should be allocated with short- and long-term goals in mind – with 60 per cent invested in long-term brand building and 40 per cent in short-term sales activation. This is required to achieve optimal results and obtain a powerful drive of sustained business success.[2]

- *B2B and B2C marketing spend:* A correlation doesn't always exist between the top 10 brands and marketing spend. For example, in 2021, Proctor and Gamble was the largest advertiser globally, having invested USD $8.1 billion. Amazon, the fourth top global brand, was the second on that list with an ad spend of USD $4.8 billion, while Unilever closed the top three with USD $4.7 billion.[3] For companies expanding globally, knowing what budget to allocate to marketing strategies and building a brand is challenging. However, as a guide for B2B and B2C industries, approximately 7.8 per cent and 15.1 per cent of revenue respectively is allocated to marketing budgets. [4]

The essentials of global branding strategies

April White is CEO of The Trust Agency, a public relations firm in the United States. April is a three-times award-winning communications specialist, official TEDx speaker and published author. During a conversation with April, I was interested in learning the essential components of creating a global branding strategy.

April shared that in the ever-evolving business landscape, a few fundamental principles stand tall, guiding brands towards success in a global marketplace. The first of these principles is authenticity, the bedrock of trust in your brand. In today's world, the public demands more than words; they demand action. According to April, telling a compelling story is not enough; you must live it.

I explored this further with April, and she provided the analogy that writers often hear the advice to 'show, not tell', and the same wisdom applies to brands. Your brand values and narrative should permeate every aspect of what you do. When your brand's actions align seamlessly with your core values, you gain something invaluable – trust. Authenticity becomes your hallmark. Conversely, attempting to convince your audience of something you're not or standing for values you don't uphold will only lead to scepticism and distrust.

Creating an emotional bond with your customers is the second principle that April and I discussed. You must deeply understand their problems, values, aspirations and emotions to do this. The objective is to define and articulate the specific problem you're solving; this is all about discovering your purpose. Your 'why' is your purpose and becomes the heart of your storytelling, attracting employees, investors, clients and partners. Your 'why' also serves as the corner-stone of your unique value proposition (UVP) – the central essence of differentiating your company's brand.

In April's experience, a brand's UVP is developed from metic-ulous research into its target audience. Your UVP should create an emotional connection, setting your brand apart from competitors. Importantly, this essence should be consistent throughout every interaction stakeholders have with your company.

I explored with April how scaleups and growth companies can build their brands as they enter new markets. April revealed that con-sistency in message and action is vital when communicating across multiple markets. While certain aspects of your brand may adapt to be localised, some elements must remain consistent for global recog-nition. Your brand's core values should shine through, transcending borders and cultural differences. This unwavering commitment to your principles portrays integrity and elevates your brand to a glob-ally respected symbol.

Exploring global expansion further with April, she explained that fostering positive relationships is the cornerstone of expansion. As your target audience diversifies, it's crucial to forge strong connec-tions that transcend geographical boundaries. Your brand should not exclusively exist as a provider of a specific solution, for example, but potentially as a global leader in shaping new and innovative ideas for the industry if it aligns with your vision and values. Consider the identity you want to craft and the perception you wish to instil.

Ultimately, no matter how prolific your brand's presence, it must consistently deliver value to customers, which comes back to under-standing your UVP.

Developing a global brand strategy

A common question from leaders as they move into global markets is whether brand or marketing comes first. A way to think about this is that branding *defines* who you are, while marketing is *building awareness* of who you are.

As a business expands internationally, establishing a recognisable brand becomes crucial for several reasons. A well-defined brand helps differentiate your company from competitors, creates a sense of trust and credibility among customers, and facilitates brand loyalty and, ultimately, profitability.

Leaders scaling globally may already have an established brand and successful marketing strategy in their current market. However, while these provide a strong foundation for global expansion, you must invest time and resources to review your brand and marketing strategy to ensure they reflect the target market.

You must do more than transplant your existing brand into a new market. Positioning your brand requires adapting to diverse cultural, linguistic and regional requirements. You need to consider local trends and opinions and engage customers personally to ensure you create an effective strategy that resonates with your future audience to build loyalty and credibility.

Unfortunately, with restricted budgets, leaders often overlook reviewing their brands before scaling and instead focus on marketing; however, this comes with a high risk. Even multinationals make mistakes translating their brand as they launch into new markets. Consider Kentucky Fried Chicken's famous slogan 'Finger Lickin' Good'. When it launched in China in the 1980s, this translated as 'Eat your fingers off'. Pepsi's slogan 'Pepsi brings you back to life' debuted in China as 'Pepsi brings you back from the grave'. In another example, Mercedes-Benz entered the Chinese market under the brand name 'Bensi', – which means 'rush to die'.[5]

As the leader of a scaleup or growth company, you will have an established brand and marketing framework implemented in your current market; therefore, the following steps will be familiar to you. However, it is critical for you to review your existing brand and marketing strategy through a new lens, focused on a new target market. I highly recommend engaging a marketing professional in the target market to ensure your strategy is aligned culturally to achieve credibility, loyalty and engagement.

Step 1: Define your brand strategy

In chapter 8, I discussed your go-to-market strategy, and defining your business's core values, vision and mission. Defining your target audience and tailoring your messaging to resonate with their needs and aspirations is crucial in building a brand to set you apart from competitors.

Define your audience in the target market

Identifying and understanding your target audience in any market is the foundation of effective branding. By defining your target audience, you can tailor your brand messaging to speak directly to their interests, preferences and pain points in foreign countries. You can begin to define your target audience by:

1. *Conducting market research:* Gather data on your potential customers in each new market. Understand their demographics, psychographics, behaviours and preferences. This research can be done through surveys, interviews and customer data analysis.

2. *Creating buyer personas:* Detailed buyer or customer personas should represent your ideal customers based on your research. Typically, these personas should capture key demographics – including age, gender, occupation and interests. However, as a word of caution, the following examples demonstrate that looking at demographics only can sometimes lead to the wrong outcome:

   - King Charles: Male, born in 1948, raised in the United Kingdom, married twice, lives in a castle, wealthy and famous.
   - Ozzy Osbourne: Male, born in 1948, raised in the United Kingdom, married twice, lives in a castle, wealthy and famous.

   Your client personas must capture not only demographics but also their pain points, problems and challenges. Where do they require support? How are you going to solve their problems and challenges? With a clear picture of your target audience, you can craft relevant and impactful messaging.

3. *Segmenting your audience:* If your target audience is diverse, consider segmenting them into smaller groups based on shared characteristics or needs. This allows you to create tailored messaging for each segment, which can increase the chances of resonating with them.

Identify your UVP

A UVP communicates your brand's benefits or advantages compared to competitors. It sets you apart from competitors in your target market, makes your brand compelling to your target audience and reinforces why they should prefer you over others. Here's how you can establish your UVP:

- *Identify competitive advantages:* The competitors in your target market will likely differ from your market of origin. Analyse your competitors and identify what separates your brand. Consider product features, quality, pricing, customer service and reputation. Pinpoint the strengths that give your brand a competitive edge.

- *Define the unique benefits:* Determine the unique benefits or value your target audience derives from choosing your brand. This could be related to convenience, innovation, sustainability, personalisation, product features such as quality, pricing or service, or other factors that make your brand stand out. What's important here is to identify how your brand emotionally connects with your current and future clients.

- *Craft a compelling statement:* Condense your unique benefits into a concise and compelling statement communicating your UVP. This statement should be memorable. It must resonate with your target audience.

Develop a clear brand positioning statement

Once you have defined your target audience and value proposition, the final step in this stage is to succinctly describe how you would like your brand to be perceived in the minds of your target audience.

It communicates the unique value you provide and your position in the market. Crafting a compelling brand positioning statement integrates your target audience and critical competitive differentiators into a concise and impactful statement that conveys the essence of your brand. The most impactful brand positioning statements are clear, unique and memorable.

Remember, these elements may evolve over time. It's essential to regularly review and refine your target audience, messaging, value proposition and positioning as your business, customer needs and market dynamics change.

Step 2: Develop a brand architecture

A well-structured brand architecture ensures consistency across all touchpoints, reinforces brand identity and improves recognition. This includes designing your visual identity, such as logos, colour scheme and typography, to reflect your brand's personality. It is also essential to develop brand guidelines and make this available to teams with external-facing roles such as client support and sales, and to external partners, including your public relations and website developer, to ensure consistency across all channels.

A strategy often overlooked during brand architecture development is identifying and appointing key opinion leaders. These individuals are high-profile, respected individuals with established, extensive networks within your industry. They are powerful advocates and can foster introductions to their networks in your new market. Selecting and cultivating your relationship with a key opinion leader will take time; however, they offer invaluable inroads to close-knit business communities.

Step 3: Craft a compelling brand story

Crafting a compelling brand story is a powerful way to engage your audience, differentiate your brand and create a lasting memorable impression. A well-crafted brand story communicates your value proposition and reflects your brand's personality and aspirations.

Two core elements need to be considered to craft a brand story. First, every brand has a journey. For growth companies with limited budgets, it is crucial to identify and articulate your journey. Consider the origins of your brand, the challenges you've overcome and the milestones you've achieved. Highlight key moments or experiences that have shaped your brand's evolution. This narrative arc will add depth and authenticity to your brand story.

The other element is your customer's journey. Map the buyer's touchpoints in your process and identify the pain points. For each persona, tailor your messaging to specifically align with their needs. The goal is to provide your customers with a positive, memorable experience at each touchpoint of their journey.

JOHN LEWIS & PARTNERS

As an example of this, each year leading up to Christmas, John Lewis & Partners Department Store in the United Kingdom releases a video. Since 2007, their award-winning videos signal the countdown to Christmas, with the release highly anticipated worldwide. The brand strategy is nostalgia, with powerful visuals and few or no words; instead, a popular song tells the story. What resonates with the audience is the emotional storyline, capturing the hearts of their audience.

What makes these videos successful is that despite being advertisements for their department store, only a simple tagline is used at the end of each video, reflecting a key brand message. For example, 'The Man on the Moon' video from 2015 ends with the simple tagline, 'Show someone they're loved this Christmas'. It refers to the ad's plotline – a young girl trying her best to communicate with a man living alone on the moon. This video received 22 million views in its first week. The more recent videos have accompanied product awareness campaigns of toys and characters featured with their hashtags, physical toys and landing pages. The John Lewis & Partners Department store is an excellent example of developing a brand strategy that, over the long term, has created memorable campaigns, delivering profits.

Step 4: Build brand awareness to foster engagement

Professor Philip Kotler famously developed the 4Ps of marketing, which he outlined as product, price, place and promotion. In recent years, a fifth P has been added – people. This 5Ps marketing framework is a cost-effective approach to execute your brand strategy and remain focused on achieving your company's goals. As your business becomes more sophisticated with its brand strategies and increased budgets, additional Ps, including process, partners and packaging, can be adopted.

The 5Ps framework is integral in driving short-term sales results in a new global market. When entering unfamiliar territories, businesses must establish their brand presence and build recognition and loyalty among the target audience. Here are some ways marketing can support this process:

- *Market research:* Marketing begins with thorough market research. Understanding the new global market's demographics, cultural nuances, consumer behaviour and competitors is essential. This may sound repetitive from your brand research, but this knowledge helps marketers tailor their strategies to position the brand and effectively resonate with the local audience.

- *Visual identity:* Marketing ensures the brand's visual identity, including logo, colours, typography and overall design, is developed and consistently applied across various marketing channels. A visually appealing and cohesive brand identity enhances brand recall and helps consumers associate specific visual cues with the brand.

  Also, I advise leaders to audit their external-facing social media, website and collateral at this stage. For example, your website must reflect a global business that is culturally aware and reflective of your target market. In-market experts must vet your tagline to ensure it conforms with your business values – and doesn't unknowingly associate with political, religious or other movements that don't align with your brand. It is this level of detail that is critical as you focus on the target market.

- *Localisation:* As previously outlined, your marketing requires localisation to succeed in a new market. Marketing materials should be adapted to the local language, cultural norms and preferences. This includes translating content, adjusting visuals and customising campaigns to ensure they resonate with the target audience. Localisation demonstrates an understanding of – and respect for – the local culture and facilitates better brand connection.

- *Digital marketing:* We operate businesses in a digital, highly connected era. Marketing tactics such as search engine optimisation (SEO), social media marketing, content marketing, email marketing and paid advertising can effectively reach and engage your audience in new markets.

  For example, I worked with an Australian client who noticed her local clients primarily sought information on Instagram, including product features and customer feedback. However, after researching the industry in the United States, we ascertained that Facebook was the primary channel used by her target clients, requiring a new strategy to develop her business brand through this new channel.

  Developing informative, engaging and relevant content to educate and engage your target audience is the goal of your brand strategy. Utilise appropriate channels such as blogs, white papers, social media and webinars to establish expertise, credibility and thought leadership within your industry.

- *Influencer marketing:* Partnering with influential individuals or key opinion leaders in the new market can significantly boost brand awareness. Collaborating with local influencers with an engaged following and strong influence can help introduce the brand to their audience and leverage their credibility and trust.

- *Public relations:* Public relations efforts can generate media coverage to raise brand awareness in the new market. Building relationships with local journalists and relevant media outlets can help the brand secure coverage, share success stories and shape its reputation in the new market.

Finally, your brand story is not static – it can evolve and adapt over time. As your brand grows and changes, update your story to reflect new milestones, achievements or shifts in your market. Continuously seek feedback from your audience and adapt your storytelling to meet their evolving needs and expectations.

Measuring the effectiveness of your marketing strategy

Measuring your brand in a new market is crucial for your business's long-term success and growth. Evaluating brand awareness, customer perception, brand equity and financial performance provides valuable insights into the overall health and impact of your marketing strategies.

Brand awareness

Brand awareness refers to the extent to which a target audience recognises and remembers a brand. As seen with the John Lewis & Partners Department Store Christmas videos, creating memorable stories is crucial in building a brand, and this takes time to develop. To measure brand awareness, businesses can employ various metrics and methods:

- *Surveys and interviews:* Conducting market research surveys and interviews can help gather data on brand recognition. By asking questions about brand recall or showing respondents visual cues such as logos or slogans, businesses can gauge brand awareness among their target audience.

- *Website analytics:* Tracking website traffic and analysing metrics such as the number of unique visitors and how many convert to sales, page views and number of referral sources can provide insights into reach and engagement. Monitoring search engine visibility and keyword rankings can also indicate brand visibility in online search results.

- *Social media reach:* Analysing social media metrics, such as followers, likes, shares and impressions, helps businesses assess the reach and impact of their brand on platforms such as Facebook, Instagram, Twitter and LinkedIn.

Customer perception

Customer perception revolves around how customers view and experience a brand. It involves assessing their satisfaction, loyalty and overall impression. Here are some methods to measure customer perception:

- *Customer surveys:* Implementing customer satisfaction surveys, such as net promoter score (NPS) or customer satisfaction (CSAT) surveys, enables businesses to collect feedback directly from customers. These surveys help gauge customer sentiment, identify improvement areas and track perception changes.

- *Online reviews and ratings:* Monitoring online review platforms, such as Yelp, Google reviews or industry-specific review sites, helps you understand customer experiences and sentiments toward your business. Analysing ratings, reviews and comments helps you to identify strengths and weaknesses and promptly address customer concerns.

- *Social media monitoring:* Paying close attention to social media conversations and mentions provides real-time insights into customer sentiment and allows for proactive customer engagement. Monitoring hashtags, brand mentions and comments can help you gauge customer perception and address any issues promptly.

Brand equity

Brand equity represents the value and strength of a brand in the marketplace. It encompasses tangible and intangible assets such as brand reputation, customer loyalty, and perceived brand value. These methods can be used to measure brand equity:

- *Brand audits:* Brand audits evaluate elements, including visual identity, messaging, positioning and brand associations. These audits help assess brand consistency, awareness and customer perception. Qualitative research methods, such as focus groups and interviews, can be employed to gain deeper insights into brand equity.

- *Customer loyalty programs:* Tracking customer retention rates, repeat purchases and referral rates can indicate the level of customer loyalty and advocacy. You can measure the success of loyalty programs for your business by monitoring program engagement, redemption rates and customer feedback.

- *Brand value assessments:* Assessing the financial value of a brand can provide insights into its overall strength and impact. Methods such as brand valuation models, including Interbrand's Best Global Brands or Brand Finance's Brand Strength Index, use financial and non-financial indicators to estimate the value of a brand.

Financial performance

Developing a brand that is memorable requires investment and considerable time for branding to resonate with the target audience. Financial performance serves as a tangible indicator of the effectiveness of a brand strategy and its impact on the bottom line. It is important to attribute financial performance to marketing activity, which is typically sales and short-term focussed, and profitability to brand performance. Key metrics to measure financial performance include:

- *Revenue growth:* Analysing revenue trends over time helps assess the impact of brand initiatives on sales results and market share. Comparing revenue growth to industry benchmarks provides a relative measure of brand performance.

- *Profit margins:* Tracking profit margins, such as gross or net profit margin, enables you to evaluate the efficiency and profitability of your business operations. Improvements in profit margins can indicate the effectiveness of branding and marketing efforts.

- *Market share:* Monitoring market share provides insights into a brand's competitive position. By tracking changes in market share over time, you can assess the effectiveness of your business's brand strategy and market positioning.

It's important to note that measuring brand effectiveness requires a combination of qualitative and quantitative methods. While quantitative data provides financial and other numerical insights, qualitative research methods such as focus groups, interviews and customer feedback offer a deeper understanding of customer perceptions and experiences.

Businesses can comprehensively view their brand's effectiveness by regularly evaluating brand awareness, customer perception, brand equity and financial performance. These insights can inform strategic decisions, help identify areas for improvement, and guide the allocation of resources to strengthen the brand and drive business growth in the long run.

***

Building a strong brand and supporting brand awareness with a rigorous research-based marketing strategy are continuous processes. They require consistent effort, adaptability and responsiveness to the evolving needs and preferences of the international market. By aligning your marketing strategies with your company's core values and consistently delivering on promises, your business can establish a robust brand presence to support successful international expansion.

Top 5 insights from this chapter

1. Global branding can be defined as the strategy companies use to communicate their values and identity in a new market.

2. Successful brands understand how to manage the tension between short-term strategies to yield quick results, such as immediate sales boosts, and long-term marketing strategies to build their brand.

3. Global branding strategies should strive to maintain consistency, foster positive, memorable relationships and deliver financial value.

4. Companies can establish their global presence through a range of tactics, such as content optimisation, brand ambassadors, key opinion leaders, local partnerships and community engagement, and developing a public relations plan.

5. When expanding your brand's presence on a global scale, it is beneficial to seek the expertise of a locally based marketing agency that is aware of trends and practices.

APPLYING
LEARNINGS
TO YOUR
BUSINESS

Self-reflection: What assumptions are you making about your brand's target audience in international markets? How can you substantiate these assumptions? Where are the gaps?

PART IV

THE TOP FIVE GLOBAL MARKETS

I n this part, I take you on a journey through the top five global markets that are instrumental in driving international expansion. The chapters are dedicated to capturing the wisdom and expertise of industry professionals who possess an intimate understanding of these key markets: Australia, the United States, the United Kingdom, Singapore and Japan. By providing interviews with experts who live and work in each market, this part offers invaluable insights into the nuances of history, culture and leadership, and provides essential lessons for leaders considering these markets.

Chapter 11 delves into the vibrant market of Australia. Through engaging interviews with experienced professionals deeply rooted in the Australian business landscape, you can gain a comprehensive understanding of the country's historical context, unique cultural dynamics and business practices. The experts included shed light on the challenges and opportunities that arise when expanding into Australia, including managing the tyranny of distance, and offering indispensable advice on leadership approaches, market entry strategies, and the importance of building strong relationships within the local business community.

In chapter 12, I shift focus to the United States, a global powerhouse that continues to attract businesses seeking international expansion, despite its complexities. Drawing on the wisdom of seasoned experts based in the United States, this chapter uncovers the rich historical tapestry, diverse cultural landscape, and complex business environment of the country. I provide exclusive insights into successful market entry strategies, navigating legal and regulatory frameworks and harnessing the entrepreneurial spirit that permeates the American business landscape.

Chapter 13 focuses on the United Kingdom. I include interviews with influential leaders residing and operating in the United Kingdom, illuminating the historical significance, cultural nuances and business climate that define this market. By delving into the experiences of these experts, you can gain a deeper understanding of how to navigate a crowded market with the leadership attributes, negotiation strategies and market-specific considerations necessary for thriving in the British business landscape.

In chapter 14, I explore the dynamic market of Singapore, known for its strategic location, pro-business environment and cultural heritage. Interviews with experts entrenched in the Singaporean market provide invaluable insights into the country's unique blend of traditions, business customs and regulatory frameworks. By examining the experiences of these professionals, you can discover the keys to successful market entry, effective networking and developing strong partnerships within Singapore's thriving business ecosystem.

The final chapter in this part immerses you in the fascinating world of Japan, a nation renowned for its rich history, technological innovation and distinctive business practices. Interviews with experts intimately familiar with the Japanese market unveil the intricate tapestry of cultural norms, leadership styles and business etiquettes that underpin success in this market. Through these experiences and this expertise, you can gain essential knowledge on building trust, establishing long-term relationships and navigating the complexities of doing business in Japan.

By capturing experts' insights and wisdom in these top five global markets, the chapters in this part help equip you with a comprehensive understanding of the historical, cultural and business contexts that shape success in these regions. The firsthand accounts and expert perspectives in this section empower you to make informed decisions, adopt effective strategies, and build meaningful relationships as you embark on global expansion efforts in these key markets.

CHAPTER 11

AUSTRALIA:
Fighting the tyranny of distance

Quick facts

Australia comprises a mainland continent, the island of Tasmania, and numerous smaller islands. General market information for Australia includes the following:

- Form of government: Federal parliamentary democracy; Commonwealth realm
- Capital: Canberra
- Population (at the time of writing): 26,402,781
- Official language: English
- Currency: Australian dollar
- Area: 7,692,024 square kilometres (2,969,907 square miles)
- Nominal GDP for 2023: USD $1.708 trillion
- GDP per capita for 2023: USD $64,964
- GDP, purchasing power parity (PPP) in 2023: USD $1.718 trillion

Australia's new foreign policy was introduced in early 2017 and established a framework for the country's economic, security and foreign policy connections. Due to low entry fees and simplified procedures, the country is recognised as the 14th best country in the world for establishing a business.

Australia's economy is a highly developed mixed economy. It is one of the wealthiest Asia-Pacific countries and has enjoyed more than two decades of economic expansion. The following major industries have greatly contributed to its economy:

- minerals and fuels
- manufacturers
- services
- rural goods
- other goods.

Australia is an attractive partner for business and investment operations due to its intellectual resources, commercial emphasis and collaborative approach. International businesses can work with Australian research institutes, invest in or incorporate Australian solutions into their current goods, or form joint ventures to promote their products internationally. Australia is ranked high in several different categories, including:

- ranking 15th as the world's most entrepreneurial country
- ranking in the top 10 among the Organisation for Economic Co-operation and Development (OECD) member nations for its total expenditure on research & development (R&D)
- coming in fifth in a ranking of the world's top 200 universities by five key subject fields.

Australia is also recognised for its involvement in cutting-edge research, with Australian research findings regularly cited in many of the world's leading publications. And it is home to world-class research institutions, modern ICT infrastructure and a well-educated workforce.

The policies of the Australian government promote foreign investment and acknowledge the numerous advantages of such investment. They offer many advantages compared with other countries seeking foreign investment, including:

- constant economic expansion

- highly qualified labour force
- strategically placed
- robust governmental and judicial systems
- dependable infrastructure.

According to the World Investment Report created by the United Nations Conference on Trade and Development (UNCTAD), Australia received the 15th most foreign direct investment (FDI) stock globally in 2021. The top Australian industries that attract foreign direct investment include:

- mining and quarrying
- real estate activities
- financial and insurance activities
- manufacturing
- wholesale and retail trade
- information and communication.

For more information on the details included here, you can access the following resources:

- www.globalpeoservices.com
- www.futureinaustralia.com
- www.austrade.gov.au
- www.ceoworld.biz
- www.dfat.gov.au
- www.oecd-ilibrary.org
- www.abs.gov.au
- www.usnews.com.

***

In the south-eastern corner of Oceania, Australia may be geographically isolated, but its commercial connections to the world, both nearby in the Asia-Pacific region and further afield, are inextricably linked.

And many business leaders have found that on the other side of long-haul flights, opportunities abound for those willing to embrace – and understand – Australia's appeal as a place where inno-vation, entrepreneurialism and, of course, its sought-after lifestyle meet, especially in the country's major cities of Sydney, Melbourne, Adelaide, Brisbane, Hobart and Perth.

Its postcard-perfect beaches and remote natural wonders contrast with vibrant inner-city business districts, with cities such as Melbourne regularly appearing in the upper echelons of The Economist Intelligent Unit's Global Liveability Index. Even after COVID-19, which brought some of the world's most strict lockdowns to the city, Melbourne often makes the top 10 – taking out third spot (with Sydney in fourth) as recently as 2023.[1] These liveability rankings, which measure the quality of infrastructure, healthcare, education and stability, highlight the uniquely favourable conditions for businesses looking to new markets.

Australia is a multicultural society, with residents and expats hailing from many corners of the world. After English, Mandarin is the second most commonly spoken language; however, the popula-tion and its business landscape are diverse. The most recent statistics (from April 2022) show that 29.1 per cent of its population was born overseas; by country of birth, England ranks first, followed by India, China and New Zealand.[2]

Founders and business leaders who are looking to expand into Australia should also be aware of the country's Indigenous heritage. It is customary for many businesses to show their respect to First Nations Peoples of Australia, who are the land's first storytellers and Traditional Owners. At a societal and professional level, this is known as an Acknowledgement of Country, which is a statement that should be included in communications in person and online. For example, an Acknowledgment of Country could be delivered as a statement at the beginning of a speech or published on company websites. Organisations such as Reconciliation Australia also provide useful guidance on the proper language and ways to acknowledge the Traditional Owners of the land.[3]

International business landscape

The country continent of Australia is well connected in terms of trade to the world, with an extensive (and growing) list of free trade agreements in place with key Asia-Pacific countries such as Japan, Malaysia, Singapore and China, to name but a few, as well as major trading partners such as the United Kingdom and the United States.[4]

A recent Australian Bureau of Statistics report charted the economic activity of foreign-owned businesses operating in Australia, and found 9946 majority foreign-owned businesses, most of which hail from the United States, the United Kingdom and Japan. According to the report, the main industries span wholesale trade, professional, scientific and technical services, financial and insurance services and manufacturing. These sectors make a significant contribution to the Australian economy and its industry value add (IVA) – especially mining (AUD $39 billion), manufacturing (AUD $29.3 billion) and professional, scientific and technical services (AUD $27.6 billion).[5]

From fintech to fashion, the influences of global businesses are certainly visible in Australia. Over the past decade, the digital age has also brought Australia closer to the world than ever before – making it easier to overcome one of the biggest challenges this market faces: its geographic distance from other countries. These digital tools have helped founders and their workforce contingents build relationships, test the market before establishing local subsidiaries, reach customers and work with international offices in other times zones with greater ease.

The technology opportunity

Australia is a tech-savvy market – and it's not just the home-grown unicorns such as Atlassian, Canva and global fintech Airwallex that demonstrate its technological prowess.

Cloud-based file sharing platform Dropbox entered the Australian market in 2014, brought over by a dedicated 'landing team' who were tasked with setting up the local Sydney office before returning to the

San Francisco headquarters. Australia was the second point of expansion for the US-based company after Dublin, Ireland in 2012.[6]

Head of Customer Success, David Chilver, who joined Dropbox in 2016, says that signs for a successful expansion into Australia were already in play, because the platform had already cultivated a local customer base. 'The company was confident that it was a strong market fit, and we were obviously fulfilling a need,' says David. 'And in 2014, we had a plan to launch the business version of the product. So that gave [Dropbox] the momentum to expand into APAC. Sydney was the first location in that region. We've since expanded into Japan and Singapore, which were very fast following from Australia.'

Before the Sydney office was opened, the landing team travelled to Australia on a 'recce' mission, meeting with other technology companies that had expanded in the market, as well as local organisations such as commerce chambers, as part of the company's process in validating the need for a physical office presence. 'The landing team actually started working Australian hours while they were in San Francisco, before they headed over so they could start to build up a pipeline and continue to engage with those customers. And when they arrived, it was solely a go-to market office.'

Dropbox then localised in Australia – first, by meeting directly with its customers including SMEs, which were the platform's core user base, followed by thought leadership communication, tailored specifically to the needs of the Australian businesses it served. A small but pivotal detail that also set up Dropbox for success in the market was selling its paid-for services in Australian dollars. 'It took away the fluctuation of the US dollar. We put proper processes around invoicing in Australian dollars,' says David. This also included components such as general sales tax (GST), Australia's nationally implemented goods and services tax.

For David, overcoming perceived disadvantages (such as Australia's far-away location from large markets such as the United States and the United Kingdom) is ultimately about looking for the opportunities instead. 'I think [Australia] does seem closer. The shift to virtual working means that things can connect on different ends of the day and into different regions. Australia is a long way away, but it gives you some opportunities you don't get when working in America.

'We are a smaller market. But we're advanced in terms of tech and cloud adoption. [Australia] is more able to think about digital first. You can also experiment in the Australian market,' he added. 'We have a high-tech literacy and it's English speaking. So that works well for not having to translate websites, for example. We have a smaller population, so you can make a global change, test it here and then roll it out.'

> We have a high-tech literacy and it's English speaking. So that works well for not having to translate websites, for example. We have a smaller population, so you can make a global change, test it here and then roll it out.

The US-based payment and modern card issuing platform Marqeta similarly noticed Australia's receptiveness to technology, expanding into the market in 2020. Having already entered Europe and delivered products and services in North America, Australia was also a natural choice. 'It is a market that is sophisticated in payments, and the infrastructure is very good,' says Melissa Keir, VP of Global Expansion at Marqeta. Australia has, according to studies, been recognised as a global leader in the uptake of new tech-driven services, such as contactless card payments, and more.[7]

Marqeta prepared for its arrival in Australia before COVID-19 restrictions were put in place, giving its leaders the opportunity to glean vital local insights, as well as how its relevant partners and global operators such as Visa and Mastercard function in the market. Melissa says part of this research was focused on listening to their perspectives on the payment sector, including what's changing and what to be mindful of. 'In order for us to offer our products and services, we needed a Banking Identification Number (BIN) sponsor. So, we were able to meet with potential sponsors locally,' said Melissa.

To be able to effectively service the Australian market from long distances, certain business activities need to be arranged locally to overcome potential challenges that could mean delays for customers or disruptions to the quality of the service provided. Marqeta established itself in Melbourne with a local subsidiary and employees, and partnered with third parties for local card distribution services within Australia to produce its physical payment cards. 'You definitely need that local, physical [card fulfilment] because you don't want to be shipping from the US,' added Melissa.

As far as other market entry and localisation activities go, Marqeta's approach retains its global proposition with market-specific communications. 'We do have a local website. And that allows us to talk about what's relevant and what's being offered [in Australia],' said Melissa.

While Australians do champion 'made in Australia', there has always been a strong appetite in the market for global brands. These have a presence in many corners of the economy, and can be seen everywhere from the news media to fast-moving consumer goods and luxury goods.

The New York Times opened a Sydney bureau in 2017, hiring a team of primarily local reporters to cover Australia and the region surrounding it through the global lens the publication is known for. Its arrival was a digital one – and makes a statement about Australia's growing connectedness to the world. In a statement explaining the rationale behind its expansion, the publication said: '... because we have a significant number of digital subscribers in the country; and because Australia, New Zealand and the Pacific all offer a rich vein of reporting in a part of the world that is increasingly important.' The publication was clear in its intention to retain its US origins and 'style', referencing dollars in USD and miles instead of kilometres. But the globally renowned brand demonstrated its ability to localise where it counts, balancing coverage of local issues with globally relevant news. Its subscriber base doubled after its first year in the market.[8]

International influence

One thing Australia can attribute, at least partly, to its international society both culturally and in terms of business is its (often enterprising) migrant population. Since Federation in 1901, when six self-governed colonies united to form the Commonwealth of Australia, the country has seen permanent migrants arrive from the United Kingdom, Italy, Greece, China and New Zealand, to name just a few of those listed in the Australia Bureau of Statistics census of individuals by birthplace. In the decades following Federation, international businesses also had more formal support and networks to expand into the market; the British Chamber of Commerce was formed in 1910, for example, followed by the Italian Chamber of Commerce in 1922.

Gennaro Autore is one of many Italian migrants who made their way to Australia, visiting on a family holiday for the first time in 1966. 'The first trip to Australia was a little bit of an adventure by my parents,' says Gennaro of the 14,000 kilometre-long journey. The Autore family migrated permanently to Australia in 1975, bringing their entrepreneurial spirit – and style sensibilities – with them from Italy.

'Our family started importing silk scarves and ties from Como – the centre of the most sophisticated and luxurious silks. Then we moved into footwear,' recalls Gennaro. The family started selling pieces to department stores such as Myer and David Jones, which paved the way for more work in the fashion sector.

More than 40 years later, Gennaro is the founding director of the family-owned Graaf Group, and he has helped expand a number of international luxury fashion and hospitality businesses to Australia. Graaf Group brought Italian luxury brands Missoni and Brunello Cucinelli to Sydney, in a recently developed retail destination at 25 Martin Place, joining the likes of already established global labels such as Valentino and Dolce & Gabbana.

In 2022, fashion designer and 'cashmere king' Brunello Cucinelli told *The Australian* newspaper he had never been to Australia (at the time of publication in September of that year). However, it seems with a local partner such as Gennaro to license the brand and help secure prime real estate, this was no obstacle when it came to opening the first bricks and mortar boutique of Cucinelli's eponymous label in Sydney in 2023.

Global expansion is, of course, about financial readiness and a strong go-to-market strategy, which includes spotting opportunity and demand ahead of time. Many luxury brands also continue flock to Australia to tap into the Asian tourist market, which (with the exception of COVID-19 related border closures) has been an important customer base for the sector in Australia.

'So entering the Australian market, for a luxury brand that is not known enough, it's quite risky. Because the investments are quite high. And to have the right visibility, it's not that easy. So I always say to brands to be cautious, because it's not necessarily always a success. The well-known brands have an easier entry into the market,' said Gennaro. 'If we're talking about traditional stores, I think one of the most important things is location. My advice would be to definitely find a location that can work and make sure that you have enough visibility and exposure to make the brand well known.'

> If we're talking about traditional stores, I think one of the most important things is location. My advice would be to definitely find a location that can work and make sure that you have enough visibility and exposure to make the brand well known.

Overseas businesses that do not succeed in the Australian market share some common factors that contribute to their downfall, including failing to appropriately localise from a communication and business strategy perspective. Localising as part of expansion, of course, needs to be done to differing degrees depending on sector, but the assumption can be risky – for example, assuming that Australia is the same as other English-speaking countries.

As with many economies, small and medium enterprises (SMEs) comprise the majority of all businesses in Australia. In the period between 2018 and 2022, nearly 2.6 million actively trading businesses were recorded via Australian Bureau of Statistics data.[9] The industries with the largest net increase during this period included construction, professional scientific and technical services, plus transport, postal and warehousing.

From global to local

Accounting for 98 per cent of all businesses in the country,[10] SMEs were the target customers for US-based small business lending company OnDeck when it began to prepare for expansion into Australia in 2015.

The NYSE–listed online lender had enjoyed success in the United States since it was founded in 2006; however, it was interest from Australia that turned OnDeck's initial attention to the market. The leaders of the business started to do their research, and the CEO, Head of strategy and Head of Legal made the trip to Sydney.

'They met with associations and tech companies and made as many connections as they could to understand whether this was a good opportunity,' says OnDeck's COO, Charlene Batson, who joined the business three months after launching in Australia.

> ❛ They met with associations and tech companies and made as many connections as they could to understand whether this was a good opportunity.

The initial visit by OnDeck's leaders was a starting point for rigorous market research, which also included on-the-ground information-gathering. 'Leadership definitely recognised Australia had a strong economy as well, and arguably still stronger than most of the rest of the developed world. That was very positive for them. And the other thing was the willingness to use digital apps and to be online, which was very high, even in 2015, versus other countries.'

However, it was ultimately a partnership with accounting software company MYOB that cemented OnDeck's transition into Australia. 'MYOB was a very well-known, established, powerful Australian company with accounting data, and that really was the clincher,' says Charlene.

The other critical part of OnDeck's expansion was an understanding of what its specific offering as a lender would need to be in the Australian market. 'OnDeck worked with one of the bureaus to buy a load of retrospective data to help localise the credit model.'

These activities were all carried out before OnDeck opened its offices in Sydney. However, the business's expansion into the market has continued to connect itself ever more closely to the Australian business landscape; in 2022, a management buyout made the company 80 per cent locally owned and operated (which comprised OnDeck's core management group and Australian investors).

Charlene added: 'I think all of those things set everybody up really well for the strategy moving forward. And the realisation at that point that there was a very big difference between the US and Australia on a number of fronts. A portion of business was very much localised, and a portion of it was intentionally kept in the US. The first split was technology, product management, and all things engineering. All of that was managed out of the US. And then locally, it was very much the sales, the operations, the credit analysis, marketing and business development – everything that was facing a customer. I think it was the market research and the reconnaissance trip that enabled the success to happen.'

CHAPTER 12

THE UNITED STATES:
The complexity trap

Quick facts

The United States of America is a country that is often lauded for its simplicity. 'The land of the free and the home of the brave,' as the saying goes.

Here's the United States at a glance:

- Form of government: Constitution-based federal republic
- Capital: Washington D.C.
- Population (at the time of writing): 336,836,222
- Languages spoken: English, Spanish. (The United States does not have an official language.)
- Currency: US dollar
- Area: 9,857,306 square kilometres (3,805,927 square miles)
- Consists of 50 states and the District of Columbia
- Ranked first in GDP per country, with 5.95 per cent growth rate for 2021
- Nominal GDP for 2023: USD $26.854 trillion.
- GDP per capita for 2023: USD $80,083
- Real GDP (constant, inflation adjusted) reached USD $17.348 trillion in 2017

America has emerged as the world's economic, military and technological leader over the last century. The country's economic growth is fuelled by different industries. The 10 largest industries by revenue are:

- drug, cosmetic and toiletry wholesaling
- pharmaceuticals wholesaling
- new car dealers
- health and medical insurance
- hospitals
- life insurance and annuities
- commercial banking
- public schools
- supermarkets and grocery stores
- property, casualty and direct insurance.

For more information on the details included here, you can access the following resources:

- www.ibisworld.com/united-states/industry-trends/biggest-industries-by-revenue/
- www.worldometers.info/gdp/us-gdp
- www.usnews.com
- www.globalbusiness.org/about-us
- www.bea.gov

***

The pursuit of prosperity and success is a long-entrenched ideal in the United States. You've no doubt heard of this pursuit as the 'great American Dream' – the concept that anyone, regardless of background or circumstance, can achieve their goals if they are dedicated and determined, and work hard.

This is a feature of the business culture of the United States, the creative and commercial energy of which has no doubt fuelled the country's growth trajectory over the past century, including its sheer scale, size and influence as the world's largest economy.

The United States received more foreign direct investment (FDI) than any other nation in 2019 and 2020, according to International

Monetary Fund data.[1] In 2021, new FDI totalled USD $333.6 billion according to the US's Bureau of Economic Analysis, with the vast majority occurring by way of company acquisition, followed by new business establishment and expansion.[2]

The United States is widely regarded as a destination for foreign-owned enterprises and is home to some of the world's most globalised cities. According to the Kearney 2022 Global Cities Report, three US cities – New York City, Los Angeles and Chicago – were among the top 10. New York City – an ever-popular point of entry for global businesses – has retained its position at the top for five years running.

To the foreign eye, the United States has historically been regarded as a place of great promise, and its business landscape is highly international – including those locally established. In 2017, The Brookings Institution reported that 'almost half of the Fortune 500 companies were founded by American immigrants or their children.'[3]

Across the United States entrepreneurialism appears to be at an all-time high. In 2021, the US Census Bureau reported a record number of new business applications, with 5.4 million filed within its own borders. The previous record was set only a year earlier in 2020, with 4.4 million applications filed. What this suggests is that new business creation continues to shape the local landscape among and after – perhaps even driven by – the COVID-19 pandemic.

Global Business Alliance, a peak industry organisation based in Washington D.C., has long championed foreign investment in the United States, and recently studied the sectors with the greatest prevalence. Its 2020 report found that retail trade was the fastest growing sector; however, the largest sectors include manufacturing, finance and insurance, wholesale trade and banking.

There are, of course, many notable growth sectors when it comes to entering this market, and to concentrate only on the sectors just mentioned would be an oversight of the breadth of opportunity that abounds in the United States. To discover these opportunities, successful founders need to think both globally and locally – and, importantly, identify the 'gap' in the market they seek to fill.

State of entry

The US market retains an allure for overseas businesses not only because of its size and the opportunities for growth and scale that naturally go with it, but also because it's an exciting place to do business. It is home to (and a concentration of) many highly motivated and driven innovators.

Its size and influence is not to be underestimated – but from state to state, it's not a monolithic business landscape. It is made up of multiple markets and regions, and the individual GDPs of some US states are comparable to the size of entire countries. Combining data from the US Bureau of Economic Analysis and the International Monetary Fund, a recent Foundation for Economic Education article looked at the numbers.[4] California has the largest GDP, followed by Texas, New York and Florida. In terms of GDP data from 2019, the article pointed out that California's economic output was higher than that of the United Kingdom, Texas more than Canada, New York more than South Korea and Florida similar to Mexico.

While all 50 states in the United States share common federal laws, it is a country of extraordinary diversity. Each state also has its own regulatory and business norms, which are constantly evolving and changing. Additionally, tax laws are notoriously complex in the United States, and these also vary from state to state.

Even US-based companies that are looking to expand interstate must navigate these differences, including 'foreign qualification', which refers to the process of business registration in another state other than the business's native state of incorporation.

This means that international entrants must bring an especially acute awareness of the differences between each state – including selecting the state of entry that most suits the needs of the individual business. Some cities' reputations precede them, such as the tech startups of Silicon Valley and New York being a diverse (and iconic) wellspring of entrepreneurship.

A 2022 CNBC survey looked at a number of key attributes to determine which states were the most amenable for businesses, including workforce, infrastructure, cost of doing business, liveability and access to capital.[5]

To understand just how localised the differences within the US states can be, even counties within states offer insights. North Carolina, which topped CNBC's list, offers a revealing example – and also points to the value of looking hyper-locally for an opportunity in this market.

North Carolina is known for its highly talented and skilled workforce, and its investment in an initiative called the Research Triangle Region, a patchwork of 14 counties that are home to 12 colleges including three top-tier research universities (Duke University, North Carolina State University and University of North Carolina Chapel Hill).[6]

North Carolina has a low corporate tax rate (2.5 per cent) and is home to 2 million people and more than 7000 companies – 700 of which are international. But the sectors are not only limited to research – agtech, manufacturing, technology and life sciences are also key industries, to name just a few. The international business presence in the region alone is highly diverse, with companies from 22 countries present, including Italy, Japan, Switzerland, Australia and Denmark. This is just one example of how localised go-to market research needs to be when expanding into the United States.

Gemma Lloyd is the co-founder and CEO of WORK180, a Melbourne-based organisation that helps workplaces to drive and promote their gender equity efforts. WORK180 entered the UK market in 2018 and the US market in 2019. Its US expansion was driven both by WORK180's global ambitions and financial readiness, including a successful Series A funding of AUD $1 million.

'We registered in Delaware and then we set up our office and our employees in Austin, Texas. That wasn't really strategic. We actually just went out and tried to find the best person and that's just where they happened to be,' says Gemma. 'Texas is a very easy state to hire in because it has limited regulation. I don't agree with that, by the way. Obviously somewhere like California is more focused on employee rights, so that they have more complexities; likewise with New York.'

Luckily for Gemma, WORK180 is in good company – at least from a registration standpoint – in Delaware. The state is, by government design, a destination for international business, offering tax incentives, a simple incorporation process and courts designed specifically to deal with corporate legal disputes.[7] Its list of international business registrations reads like a roll call of some of the most influential companies in technology, finance, consulting and more, with the likes of InterContinental Hotels Group, Fujifilm, Accenture and AstraZeneca Pharmaceuticals among them. However, there are important differences to note when incorporating in Delaware, since some tax incentives apply only to businesses that do not conduct their business in the state. This is where rigorous research, as well as local legal and accounting partners are essential to properly establish and incorporate a business.

ASX–listed, Sydney-born Xref entered the US market in 2019 by way of Toronto, Canada, before establishing its US limited liability company (LLC) in Austin, Texas. Xref is an automated recruitment referencing software-as-a-service (SaaS) platform, and was born a global business from its inception in 2009.

CEO and co-founder Lee-Martin Seymour said, 'The reason we decided to [expand globally] is because we were already getting interest from overseas companies. We were a private business and we didn't have the cash to put behind a global expansion. We were profitable in Australia, but we just didn't have that growth capital. So that's why we listed on the stock market,' said Lee. What Xref did have, however, was a scalable capital growth mechanism that set the foundation for organic international expansion.

So how did Xref decide on which markets to expand to, and when? Because of any international referees listed on individual CVs that applicants would submit via the platform, Xref's service was already being experienced or sampled, globally. Xref used this opportunity to follow up with every referee, asking them if they would be interested in learning more. Lee said, 'If these referees in particular countries don't answer this feedback, we question, "Do we have a business there?" We've always been very successful at turning around feedback in Japan and South Africa, Canada and in the US. So we've got this crystal ball that says, "Have a look over here." or "Don't go over there." And that's really guided our hand.'

Xref also leveraged the existing trusted incumbents to assist with its entry into the highly complex US market. 'There were businesses such as Oracle and Workday, which are huge, behemoth applicant tracking systems, but they didn't have automated references. So, we integrated with companies like Bullhorn. The US is a brand economy, and we integrated with the brands that were already trusted and that had app marketplaces off the side.' This, Lee said, drove a flow of natural enquiry, where the brands could easily discover Xref via its own software package and marketplace.

Localization with a 'z'

From the perspective of other English-speaking countries, an important element of localisation is often easily overlooked – including the general business language and US English differences. Businesses should integrate small but important steps into their storytelling, marketing collateral and communications that demonstrate a true commitment to the market. This also applies at a regulatory level, which can help establish all-important local credibility. The United States may be a high-output, fast-paced market, but not at the expense of due diligence and attention to detail when it comes to establishing business infrastructure and its outward-facing identity. In short, businesses can demonstrate their commitment to the market and attention to detail by paying attention to these aspects.

'In the US, you're not going to hold someone's attention for very long if you're not a US-incorporated LLC,' added Lee from Xref. 'If your privacy policy doesn't scream US-based, if you haven't got an address shown in the United States, and if you have "organisations" without a 'z' somewhere on your website ... you cannot afford to do it. We learned that very early.'

❝ **If your privacy policy doesn't scream US-based, if you haven't got an address shown in the United States, and if you have "organisations" without a 'z' somewhere on your website ... you cannot afford to do it. We learned that very early.**

During WORK180's expansion journey into the United States, Gemma started to 'relocate' virtually before she was able to spend time there in person, while waiting for her visa and due to the COVID-19 pandemic and its travel restrictions. She says this was an invaluable trust-building part of the expansion process.

'I put in little signals to show that I'm on the ground, even when I'm not. On my email signature, I have "working Pacific Standard Time", and I have a San Francisco landline phone number that gets redirected to my mobile. Those little signals have definitely helped,' said Gemma.

Companies also need to understand their customers – and their unique needs – in the United States. As many business leaders who have successfully expanded into this market note, while your product or service may be taken to new markets, customers it serves will differ, and to varying degrees in the United States.

Almira Armstrong, founder of Atelier Lumira, a niche luxury fragrance brand, regularly visits her US retail partners as part of an ongoing process to understand and learn from those who purchase the product. Lumira's first entry point to the US market was via the then iconic department store Barneys, in New York City.

'When we felt confident that we'd established Lumira in Australia, the US was the next logical market for expansion. They have a strong niche fragrance market and, at the time, there was huge interest in the A-Beauty [Australian beauty] trend,' says Almira.

'I've also found the US is not one single market; it's made up of many markets, and they can be quite different,' says Almira. 'So while I spend time in New York and Los Angeles, it's equally important for me to visit cities like Dallas and Florida regularly. It allows me to look for marketing opportunities, speak to retailers and customers, and understand the different customer profiles and where they shop.'

Lumira is one of a growing number of product-led businesses that service the US market from outside of the country. This is a sector-specific strategy that doesn't work for every business, but it's an increasingly common way to reach customers from abroad.

'Thanks to social media, we really are living in a global retail world. When customers hear about a new product or brand, they want to try it immediately,' says Almira. 'Our own e-commerce site has been essential for giving customers around the world the opportunity to try Lumira. We've also worked very hard behind the scenes to set up distribution centres in different markets, to ensure their orders are fulfilled quickly and efficiently. It's all about putting the customer first and thinking about their needs. Serving them through our e-commerce site is the first step in this process.'

> ❛ It's all about putting the customer first and thinking about their needs.

The venture capital jungle

Many founders and entrepreneurs look to the United States for a slice of its dynamic venture capital action – which is one of the highest ranking countries in the world when it comes to startup investment.[8]

Despite the ebb and flow of market fluctuations in recent years, we can still see this in action, some three years after the beginning of the COVID-19 pandemic, elections and economic shifts, with Pitchbook's Venture Monitor, which reported USD $150.9 billion of total capital raised in the third fiscal quarter of 2022. At a federal government level, directing more capital to managers and founders has been legislated; however, the landscape is constantly changing, including implementation time lines and parameters.

California-based venture investor and advisor Jennifer Byrne has seen thousands of startup pitches throughout her career. She is co-founder and President of Quesnay, which she founded to connect young companies to market leaders in disrupted industries. Throughout her 20-year career, she has also championed women-led entrepreneurship, and is also the founder of global accelerator, Female Founders in FinTech, InsurTech & Mobility.

Jennifer's advice for foreign businesses looking to raise capital in this competitive market centres not only on rigour of localised research and pitch preparation, but also on other 'soft' skills, including how to show up to meetings with investors. Some expectations of investors are particular to the US market, and the goalposts are constantly shifting. For example, financial milestones are moving when it comes to pre-seed funding rounds, and Jennifer says that because of the competition, founders are being asked to prove more, earlier.

'Two years ago, pre-seed round two funding would expect to see founders raise less and have to prove less. But in recent years, founders are raising USD $2 million in a pre-seed round, and are being asked traction questions,' says Jennifer. These expectations are higher than normal both in terms of dollars and articulating the business strategy and proposed outcomes.

Gemma echoes the sentiment when describing taking WORK180 to the United States. She quickly realised that in order to make an impression and stand out, she needed to be comfortable talking about – and working with – larger numbers than in Australia. 'There's a big difference between a series A capital raise in the US compared to a series A in Australia,' says Gemma. 'In Australia, series A means you're looking at around AUD $1 million. In the US, it may be USD $10 million to $15 million.'

With different expectations also comes the requisite of differing behavioural approaches, which both Jennifer and Gemma say is about showing up with confidence.

'Displaying confidence backed by clear and direct communication about the problem you are solving, size of the opportunity and why you are best equipped to solve this problem is what's important, but it doesn't come naturally to non-Americans,' adds Jennifer. 'I would say to be very confident and more salesmanship-like. You have to be prepared for the cultural difference if you come to the US.'

> Displaying confidence backed by clear and direct communication about the problem you are solving, size of the opportunity and why you are best equipped to solve this problem is what's important, but it doesn't come naturally to non-Americans.

Ultimately, researching the specific investor who is in the room is an absolute necessity. Jennifer advises founders to look more closely beyond stereotypical, broad perceptions. 'Don't make assumptions because [the investor is] in Silicon Valley. Each investor is different. They might ask similar questions, but not knowing the local market, who and where they have invested in and how you stack up against American competitors could mean you have left out something they might consider really important. You have to be able to answer questions in a way that resonates with the investor who is asking the questions,' said Jennifer.

A national sport (and it's not the Super Bowl)

One of the biggest challenges foreign businesses face is the country's highly litigious society. So, in navigating the many different markets within the United States, particular attention must be paid to comply with local regulations and laws. Local, accredited legal counsel and advisors are a must – especially those who understand the unique state-to-state differences.

But more than that, regulations are constantly changing, and can be influenced by many factors, including new presidential administrations and global events, to mention just a few. These shifts can have implications for trade and corporate taxes, for example. Employers also need to make sure they hire in accordance with local labour laws. Even website and customer terms and conditions need specific market localisation from a legal standpoint – those originally created in another market may not meet the requirements on US soil. There may also be sector-specific regulations that apply to different industries, from fintech to beauty products. These are just a few key elements foreign businesses need to be aware of when entering the United States.

In addition to legal counsel and research, foreign businesses should bring in expertise to fill gaps in their own knowledge. Jennifer suggests assembling an advisory board, which can help founders avoid making costly mistakes. 'Finding a few advisors in each of the areas of discipline where you are not an expert can save time and money; for example, helping with hiring, fund raising, marketing and door opening,' says Jennifer.

Building relationships can be one of the great joys (and benefits) of doing business in the interconnected nature of the United States – and Jennifer says that there are plenty of people who may be willing to help. 'If the project is interesting enough, there are lots of people looking to support founders, in particular, underrepresented founders, or who want to give back or just work on an interesting project as a side job.'

CHAPTER 13

THE UNITED KINGDOM: Breaking through in a crowded market

Quick facts

The United Kingdom is made up of England, Wales, Scotland and Northern Ireland. (These four countries have nation status in their own right, but for the purposes of this chapter, I refer to the United Kingdom as a whole.) The United Kingdom is regarded as the birthplace of contemporary parliamentary democracy as well as the Industrial Revolution.

General market information for the United Kingdom includes the following:

- Form of government: Unitary state, Constitutional monarchy
- Capital: London
- Population (at the time of writing): 68,956,025
- Official language: English
- Currency: Pound sterling
- Area: 242,495 square kilometres (93,628 square miles)
- Nominal GDP for 2023: USD $3.16 trillion
- GDP per capital for 2023: USD $46,371
- GDP, purchasing power parity for 2023: USD $3.847 trillion

The country's economy is dominated by services industries, including:

- retail
- hospitality
- professional services
- business administration
- finance.

The main investment partners of the United Kingdom (in terms of foreign direct investment stocks) include the United States, the Netherlands, Luxembourg, Belgium, and the British offshore islands (Channel Islands and Isle of Man). Most FDI flows are directed to:

- financial services sector
- professional
- scientific and technical services
- retail and wholesale trade
- transportation and storage
- IT.

According to experimental analysis, foreign ownership made up 1.1 per cent of UK-based companies in 2018, but 13.4 per cent of all UK corporate assets. Of the assets of the foreign-owned enterprises, 19.1 per cent were held by firms with a UK-based ultimate parent (that is, UK companies investing in the United Kingdom through a foreign affiliate). In the United Kingdom, 93 per cent of foreign-owned enterprises had more than 50 per cent foreign ownership, while 7 per cent had minority foreign ownership (between 10 per cent and 50 per cent foreign ownership).

For more information on the details included here, you can access the following resources:

- www.nationsonline.org/oneworld/united_kingdom.htm
- www.imf.org
- www.bbc.com
- www.great.gov.uk
- www.unctad.org
- www.santandertrade.com
- www.ons.gov.uk

- www.gov.uk
- www.statista.com.

***

In an article that remembered Queen Elizabeth II's remarkable legacy and leadership style, *Entrepreneur* noted her 'keep calm and carry on' attitude, her pragmatism and her adaptability to change, all of which were consistently represented in her global public image throughout her 70-year reign.[1] Royalist or not, if ever there were words to describe navigating the culture and commerce of the United Kingdom, all can agree those would certainly be apt.

So what exactly does Queen Elizabeth II have to do with global business expansion? Described and celebrated as the 'only constant' throughout massive change during generations of Britons' lives, her leadership offers an insight into the cultural values of the United Kingdom. On Bloomberg.com, renowned British writer Ben Schott described her as an 'ambassador' of the most influential kind to one of the world's most iconic brands: the British Royal Family.[2] Distinct. Memorable. Defined by service to others. Steady, but ever-changing.

But for all its heritage-steeped traditions, the United Kingdom is also a dynamic market known for innovation and progress. Many global businesses look to the UK market for access to its diverse and highly skilled talent pool, stable legal and regulatory environment and the abundant opportunities for growth as a global financial centre.

Throughout its long history, like any country, the United Kingdom has endured many challenges – from wartime to political upheaval, economic downturns and public health crises. However, it has retained its global influence and relevance as a key economic centre as the sixth largest economy in the world, according to the World Bank.

A pivotal moment in recent history that has profoundly impacted international business occurred when, after 47 years of membership, the island nation made its exit from the European Union (EU). During its membership of the EU, the United Kingdom was a true business gateway to Europe. Overseas businesses were able to take advantage of the ease of movement of goods, services, capital and talent between the EU's 27 member states, with the United Kingdom as their entry point.

Since the country separated from the EU, however, the United Kingdom has retained its appeal for inbound enterprise at an international level. It is, of course, still geographically close to Europe. Even without EU ties and with regulations continuing to evolve, inbound business is still not only welcome but also actively supported and encouraged across both the public and private sectors.

With more than 70 free trade agreements in place, the United Kingdom continues to be closely connected to many economies – notably the United States, its largest trading partner. Even with the uncertainty of operating in a post-Brexit era, numerous reports point to a continued confidence from US businesses in the United Kingdom.[3] In recent years, the United Kingdom has also signed new agreements with Australia, New Zealand and, under the Eastern and Southern African countries agreement, Madagascar and Comoros.

Locally, the United Kingdom is a highly saturated, diverse and competitive market. This attribute poses one of the most challenging obstacles overseas businesses face when looking to enter. According to data from the Department for Business, Energy and Industrial Strategy, SMEs comprise 99.9 per cent of the private sector business population of 5.6 million businesses.

To paint a picture of the local competition by sector, the largest number of SMEs (16 per cent) operate in the construction industry, closely followed by professional, scientific and technical activities (15 per cent) and wholesale and retail trade and repairs (10 per cent).

The United Kingdom continues to enjoy a healthy flow of foreign businesses from a wide range of sectors and countries. According to the Office for National Statistics, the number of foreign-owned businesses increased by 5.6 per cent in recent years. The majority were European-owned; however, the data also revealed significant increases in Asian-owned businesses. The inbound industries are wide ranging, with the largest including wholesale and retail trade.

The financial services sector serves as an interesting indicator of the United Kingdom's enduring global appeal. Ernst & Young's 2022 UK Attractiveness Survey for Financial Services found that while 'financial services and foreign direct investment fell 2.8 per cent across Europe in 2021 ... the United Kingdom bucked this trend attracting seven more projects than the year before and recording a total of 63 in 2021.'[4] A similar upward trend is evident in the fintech sector. As reported by *FinTech* magazine, inbound global investment for the sector reached USD $4.1 billion in recent years, second only to the United States.[5]

A strong value proposition is especially important when breaking into this market. Because it is so saturated across many sectors, the need to articulate a point of difference – and leverage branding and communication to stand out – is even more pronounced in the United Kingdom than other commercial landscapes.

To service this communication need, the United Kingdom is also home to the largest advertising market in Europe, and the fourth largest globally, sitting behind the United States, China and Japan.[6] Research from IBISWorld also found that public relations and communications, as a sector, has grown in recent years – with the exception of a small drop during COVID-19 – by 4.2 per cent on average between 2017 and 2022.[7]

Succeeding in the UK market requires many things, but three distinct elements stand out. These include strong branding, a solid knowledge of the back-office infrastructure required to establish a business and being as specific as possible about your customer.

Nicky Valentine, managing director of Orange Square, a specialist distributor of niche and luxury fragrances, has worked in the communications and marketing industry for more than 30 years in the United Kingdom, specialising in the luxury goods sector. Nicky has worked with local and global brands throughout her career, launching products into the market, and crucially, via the media as a key stakeholder.

'The UK market is a bit more conservative than most, and it's a sophisticated market as well. In the UK, you have to find that real story thread, insight or hook that is unique to whoever you're talking to,' says Valentine. 'You really can't regurgitate something that's happened globally. Audiences want something that is very UK first.'

> The UK market is a bit more conservative than most, and it's a sophisticated market as well. In the UK, you have to find that real story thread, insight or hook that is unique to whoever you're talking to.

Nicky says customers in the United Kingdom are constantly striving for something new, innovative and authentic. One way brands and businesses are achieving this is through partnerships and collaborations that leverage mutually beneficial, existing brand reputations to create something unique.

Long-term planning is also key in a crowded market like the United Kingdom. Capturing attention with a unique, bold campaign, branding and communications is one thing – but it's quite another to retain it.

'You have to have a long, strategic plan. Think about how to orchestrate your community. You can have a really great story but if you tell it all in one go, you won't be able to sustain engagement,' adds Nicky. 'Businesses need to really think what their cut through and point of difference story is. It can be quite niche, and then it can grow.'

Ultimately, branding and communication in the United Kingdom is about standing out – especially with the emerging Gen Z population, who will also be the future leaders of many brands and businesses. 'Businesses have to be brave. The new younger consumer is looking for something super unique,' says Nicky.

Bringing back-office functions to the forefront of global expansion

When entering any market, back-office infrastructure is essential. In the United Kingdom, attaining basic business necessities such as a local bank account can be arduous and time-consuming without the proper advice and entry strategy – especially for foreigners.

Bobby Lane, founder of London-based business Factotum, has also seen the power – and necessity – of branding and communication in such a crowded market. So much so, that marketing is a core function of his business, alongside the HR, payroll, IT and accounting services it provides. As a chartered accountant by profession with more than 29 years' experience, Bobby has seen how the financial health of businesses relies on the success of multiple back-office functions working in harmony.

When web advertising company and digital behemoth Taboola expanded into the United Kingdom in 2012, Bobby was called upon to help set up their accounting. Similarly, when creative and media agency VaynerMedia was looking to enter the UK market in 2015, it was Bobby who was asked to help them land.

'If a business comes to the UK, it's important that the brand is recognisable and that it's appropriate for the UK market. It also has to be visible online through social and online reviews,' says Bobby. 'It's about building your online presence, your branding, your social media presence and being accessible and visible across multiple marketing platforms.'

Again, this is with the Gen Z talent pipeline in mind, who are digital natives and currently represent approximately 20 per cent of the UK population. By 2029, they will also be the largest generational cohort in the United Kingdom.

Successfully entering the UK market is also defined by less tangible, but equally important, cultural elements, including everything from office location to more personal considerations for business leaders, such as local schools and – as Bobby says with humour – knowing which football team to support.

Bobby's team works with both local and international brands entering the UK market, including the likes of international haircare empire Sassoon. Having initially approached Factotum to assist with managing its payroll in the United Kingdom, this evolved into global accounting for the business.

The rules around taxes can also trip foreign businesses up. Bobby notes, 'Business leaders often underestimate the cost of employment, including pension contributions, tax obligations and value-added tax (VAT), which is the UK's goods and service tax.'

While it's not a legal requirement to have a UK-based (company) director, for example, it does make establishing a business more difficult if located abroad. 'A lot of people underestimate the operational nightmare of not having a local director,' says Bobby. 'For example, when you're trying to set up terms with suppliers, or open a bank account, if you've only got a director who is international, they've got to do their legal compliance checks.' This can be incredibly time-consuming and difficult to navigate without the proper advice.

> A lot of people underestimate the operational nightmare of not having a local director.

Know your niche

From media to management consulting, a stroll around key business districts such as Canary Wharf reveals the ongoing presence of large global corporates, including US-born Time Inc., Boston Consulting Group and Japan-originated Daihatsu Diesel, to name but a few. However, the United Kingdom is also home to startups and scaleup entrepreneurs from all corners of the world.

Founder and director of law practice Law Squared, Demetrio Zema is well versed in the art and business of working in multiple locations, travelling between his Sydney, Melbourne and Brisbane offices on a weekly basis. So when the time came to expand into the United Kingdom in mid-2022, it was, with the exception of a few thousand extra miles to commute, a relatively seamless transition.

Demetrio's travel agility and entrepreneurial mindset as a founder may have provided a solid foundation on which to navigate a longer distance expansion, but it was his business model as a NewLaw practitioner that helped define the success of his entry to the United Kingdom. The business offers dual-jurisdiction support and advice for Australian businesses, including privacy, data protection, technology and strategic support for in-house legal counsel teams with dual jurisdictional businesses, employees and clients.

'Our global expansion plan is to enter jurisdictions that enable us to easily replicate our model. And the two jurisdictions where we can do that are the UK and New Zealand. There are other jurisdictions of interest, but we can't do it. Singapore, for example, has different requirements where law firms must be majority owned by a local practising lawyer. The US has very similar rules.'

Legal services are not in short supply in the United Kingdom; however, Law Squared's innovative approach addresses a specific niche. 'We've gone into the UK very specifically to work with Australian companies in the UK, and UK companies in Australia,' says Demetrio. 'We have a unique offering as one firm with offices in both counties, and being a referral source rather than a competitor for existing UK law firms. Having a clear niche allows us to differentiate ourselves and capture that market of cross-border corporate clients.'

The value of hyper-local

The founders of farm management app AgriWebb conducted thorough research before entering the UK market in 2018. The agtech platform was founded in 2015 by Justin Webb, Kevin Baum and John Fargher, and was designed to help farmers to manage livestock more efficiently and sustainably. More than 16,000 farmers and ranchers now use the platform globally.

'AgriWebb was initially drawn to the UK market as a source of investment capital as opposed to a dedicated growth opportunity,' said Justin. 'As such, we acquired a local business, FarmWizard, to empower our foothold in the domestic market. From that vantage, we discovered that the UK represented a significant and valuable opportunity.'

'We didn't initially treat [this market] as a growth engine,' says Justin of AgriWebb's approach. 'We treated it as a credible testbed for the most advanced market in the world, with the most demanding customers, product fit and integrated supply chain.'

However, some obvious advantages – relevant and highly specific to AgriWebb's sector – pulled the business to the United Kingdom. 'It is the most sophisticated market for carbon sustainability and environmental footprint of food or provenance of food, from a government level down to the consumer,' says Webb.

Recognising the limitations of having a small team to begin with, AgriWebb's initial approach was also hyper-local in focus; the team went to rural Wales to engage with the local community, where AgriWebb's original customer was based.

'It's tempting for people to think of the UK as one country. But you have to really identify your core customer and what value you're going to deliver,' adds Justin, who is also a British national. 'Then, identify the greatest small pocket of density of that exact customer, and stick to it. Do not start picking core customers that sit geographically diverse. If you do pick a broad base geographically, it's almost impossible to run a small team that can cover all of these.'

While AgriWebb's story pertains more to businesses that enter the UK market with a smaller workforce, it rings true for any entity embarking on expansion with limited resources. Particularly in a crowded market such as the United Kingdom, it pays to stay focused, truly understand who you are trying to reach, and tailor your branding and communication to speak directly to them. Getting the foundations right in this market can certainly help business leaders 'keep calm and carry on'.

CHAPTER 14

SINGAPORE:
Navigating cultural heritage

Quick facts

The Republic of Singapore is a country within South-East Asia, and it is the only country from the region that has English as one of its official languages. Singapore consists of not just one island but 64. Here's Singapore at a glance:

- Government: Unitary parliamentary republic
- Location: South-East Asia, islands between Malaysia and Indonesia.
- Capital: Singapore
- Population (at the time of writing): 5,989,415
- Languages: PuTongHua (Mandarin Chinese, official), Malay (official and national), Tamil (official), English (official)
- Currency: Singapore dollar
- Area: 734.3 square kilometres (283.5 square miles)
- Nominal GDP for 2023: USD $515.548 billion
- GDP per capita for 2023: USD $91,100
- GDP, purchasing power parity for 2023: USD $757.726 billion

Singapore is a major trade, logistics and manufacturing hub for:

- aerospace
- wealth management
- financial services, including fintech

- water and waste treatment technology
- healthcare and medical, including medtech
- food and beverage services
- oil and gas
- clean energy.

Singapore's Economic Development Board (EDB) reports that more than 37,000 international companies, including 7000 multinational corporations, have their headquarters settled within the country.

Related information about Singapore foreign direct investments includes:

- Current account recorded a surplus of USD $19.9 billion in June 2022.
- Singapore direct investment abroad expanded by USD $8.7 billion in June 2022.
- Its foreign portfolio investment increased by USD $7.2 billion in June 2022

For more information on the details included here, you can access the following resources:

- www.austrade.gov.au
- www.hawksford.com
- www.demystifyasia.com
- www.ceicdata.com
- www.hashmicro.com.

***

In 1972, Singapore's then–Minister for Foreign Affairs, Sinnathamby Rajaratnam, gave a speech that would set the commercial and cultural direction for the world's only island-city-country for decades to come.

The aptly titled speech, 'Singapore: Global City', outlined Rajaratnam's vision for the future – a framework that both embraced the city's heritage and its future as a hub for inbound and outbound international business.

In doing so, the minister referenced a new type of city that was only just beginning to emerge at the time. 'They call it Ecumenopolis – the world embracing city,' he said.

Referencing the central roles of technology and innovation, an internationally connected financial network, multinational corporate attraction, and easily accessible airports and ports, he identified many key features that have come to define the Singapore of today as one of Asia's wealthiest and largest trading hubs. Rajaratnam's ideas were ahead of his time and retain their relevance to this day.

In the decades that followed, Singapore has become not only a key component of the worldwide global business system, but also a highly desirable business destination for internationally minded leaders and a crucial gateway for expansion into South-East Asia – a region that is growing with pace, relevance and investment within the broader context of global business.

The self-made city

While geographically small, contemporary Singapore has evolved into a formidable economic powerhouse in the Asia-Pacific region, and this upward trajectory began to truly take shape after 1965 when it became an independent nation.

Singapore was designed with inbound global business expansion in mind. In 2020, the World Bank identified it as the second easiest place to do business, following New Zealand.

A few factors that are especially appealing to foreign business owners include Singapore's tax incentives, including low tax on currency and other tax benefits for start-ups. It is also renowned for its strong intellectual property laws, and a robust regulatory framework that makes it a safe and trusted economy in which to operate.

According to Pew Centre research, Singapore is the most religiously diverse country in the world, and is home to Chinese, Malay, Indian, Eurasian and Peranakan (which refers to those of Chinese and Malay/Indonesian heritage) populations. In 2022, Singapore was home to 3.55 million citizens and 1.56 million non-residents, according to Statista data.[1] The city's overseas residents hail from all corners of the world including Singapore's Asian neighbours, the United States, the United Kingdom and Australia, to name but a few, making it uniquely placed to benefit from diversity of talent, culture and thought when it comes to doing business. The highly skilled, often bilingual, local talent pool is also a draw for overseas businesses – while the city actively works to attract highly skilled expats in tandem.

Dyson, for example, had Singapore's local talent in mind when it relocated its headquarters to Singapore from the United Kingdom in 2022, and actively sought expertise in the engineering and science fields, as the brand continued its growth in the region (including in Malaysia and the Philippines).[2]

Startup central

The startup economy of Singapore is especially vibrant in the technology, communications and e-commerce industries. It is home to the largest concentration of unicorns in South-East Asia, with a total of 20 recorded in 2022 (as reported by Statista).[3] Of those, 17 were part of cross-border investment activity.[4]

One technology startup success story based out of Singapore, Grab, has made localisation in eight different South-East Asian markets a key component of its global expansion strategy. It has been so successful in the Singapore market that it (to some controversy) pushed Uber out of the market.[5] Grab started as a ride-hailing app for taxis called MyTeksi in Kuala Lumpur, Malaysia, in 2012, before moving its headquarters to Singapore in 2014. Since then, Grab has evolved into a tech titan and a unicorn 'super app' that combines a range of features, from deliveries to financial services, calling itself 'The Everyday Everything App'.

When it comes to global growth in South-East Asia by way of Singapore, there appears to be an opportunity to focus on specific customer bases, if Grab's example is anything to go by. The World Advertising Research Center (WARC), a marketing data and analytics service, highlighted the future of Grab's presence in some 253 cities across the region, noting its 'hyper-local' strategy.[6] For the super app, this has meant not only rolling out local iterations such as 'GrabTukTuk' in Cambodia, but also adapting to the local regulatory requirements.

Sydney-born human resources technology platform Employment Hero, founded in 2014, offers another example of how businesses can navigate the differing systems of the region successfully – and it all began with a globally minded company design that took into account local differences between its point of entry of Singapore and the South-East Asian countries it aimed to reach.

In 2021, Employment Hero raised AUD $45 million as part of series D funding to aid its global expansion and growth in key markets, which brought its market capitalisation to AUD $250 million. The business had its sights set on growth in three markets outside of Australia: the United Kingdom, New Zealand and South-East Asia. As part of the latter, Employment Hero had already entered the Singapore and Malaysian markets.

Two key attributes to Employment Hero's global growth in the region can be noted.

Firstly, its services are built for the small- and medium-sized enterprise (SME) market, combining payroll, human resources and benefits schemes cohesively in its platform. It is not surprising that by entering South-East Asia, the potential for scalable growth is massive. According to the Asian Development Bank, in 2022 there were 71 million micro-, small- and medium-sized enterprises (MSMEs), comprising 97 per cent of all businesses in the region.

Secondly, as reported in an article by TechCrunch, Employment Hero recognised the necessity to localise from the outset in Singapore and Malaysia.[7] As part of this expansion, it tailored its employment policies and contracts in compliance with local laws and regulations.

Cultural heritage

Global influences from regions near and far have always defined the 'melting pot' of cultural and political influences in Singapore. Modern Singapore is said to have been founded when Sir Thomas Stamford Raffles arrived in 1819. Raffles saw its potential as an ideally placed trading hub – a reputation it continues to uphold to this day. Some landmarks that still stand today are a result of overseas investment, such as the iconic Raffles Hotel, founded by Armenian hoteliers the Sarkies brothers in 1887.

Expansion from overseas into Singapore is as much a part of its history as its own identity. In 1877, the Hong Kong and Shanghai Banking Corporation Limited (HSBC) opened its first Singapore branch – one of the first overseas banks to do so. Today, as mentioned, the country is home to some 37,000 international companies, 7000 of which are multinationals with regional headquarters.

While Singapore is abundant in talent and enterprise from overseas, it is also home to many intergenerational family-run companies. Overseas entrepreneurs and business leaders may find it easier to fit within the expat business crowd; however, the local nuances of Singapore must also be noted and adapted to. From a Singaporean perspective, the city strives to retain its strong sense of identity.

British-born essayist and travel writer Pico Iyer captured Singapore's diverse cultural heritage as part of the 2020 lecture series Lien Fung's Colloquium for Singapore Management University. Responding to the topic 'Remaining ourselves in the global city' Iyer said, 'When Singapore came into the world as a Republic, it very much had an Asian face, a British history all around it and a global perspective.'[8]

Iyer, who first visited Singapore in 1984, said he saw much of his own Indian ancestry reflected in its culture, and the prominent influences of other Western metropolises. 'A few years later when I moved to Japan, I noticed how much Japan and Singapore had in common in terms of discipline and order and a sense of community,' said Iyer.

Setting the business agenda

In its 2022 budget, the Singapore government identified four key pillars to fuel growth for its 'Singapore Economy 2030' vision, including services (especially those in the digital and sustainability arena), trade and enterprise. Addressing climate change and sustainability – at both a commercial and social level – continues to be a key priority for Singapore (and an opportunity many entrepreneurs have embraced).

Over the past decade alone in Singapore, much has changed and it's a city that always has its eye on the future. It's now teeming with accelerator programs, venture capital funding, government grants for startups and coworking spaces. The metaverse, e-commerce and Web3 are three sectors any foreign market entrant can expect to see increasingly more of when doing business in Singapore, with a strong appetite for innovation and 'trending' ideas and opportunities.

The government is also making it easier for expats to relocate to Singapore with its Overseas Networks and Expertise (ONE) pass, which was introduced in 2022. This particular entry pass, which has no limit on number of entrants, is part of the city's longer term plan to help attract talent after COVID-19 restrictions, which disrupted the flow of expats into the country.

A green economy

Singapore's skyline gives many clues to its commercial and environmental priorities, with sustainability a key sector. From the 'Supertrees' dotted across the Gardens by the Bay (which is home to 1.5 million species of plants), to vegetation-clad tall buildings, not only does nature coexist with businesses, but entire sectors are also being built off the back of it.

For one Australian entrepreneur living in Singapore, Elly Both, a recent meeting of global minds at the Singapore Fintech Festival was particularly revealing of the opportunities. Elly, who founded Bright Green, a sustainability consultancy, said, 'Singapore prides itself as a hotbed of innovation, attracting some of the best startup talent in the world, so I was thrilled to see this talent turning their collective minds to solve some of the biggest sustainability challenges, particularly in the fintech space. There is funding available for startups in Singapore and the focus on sustainable finance is really encouraging.'

The government-driven 'Singapore Green Plan 2030' certainly supports the opportunity that Elly observed.[9] Over the next decade, the city will continue to prioritise sustainability as part of its net-zero emissions targets.

Setting up a local entity

An Australian citizen, Elly established her business in 2020 before the COVID-19 pandemic took hold. As a Dependant's Pass (DP) holder, she says the process was relatively straightforward.

Elly says that local market knowledge and a detailed market entry strategy is, of course, essential but bringing business to Singapore also means getting the basics right, starting with business entity establishment. 'The best advice I can give in terms of setting up a business in Singapore is to engage the services of a company secretarial business to support you in navigating business registration,' said Elly. 'Do your own research and be ready to ask lots of questions to get the most out of your experience. The agency you work with should be able to give you open and honest advice on all the options available to you, and support you in deciding the right approach for you and your business needs.'

> ❛ The best advice I can give in terms of setting up a business in Singapore is to engage the services of a company secretarial business to support you in navigating business registration.

'Singapore is often considered a soft landing into Asia and, as such, the cultural impacts and differences can often be overlooked by newcomers,' she added. 'When clients are relocating into the region for the first time, I recommend they educate themselves through cultural training, and business advisory services. The Singapore Government has helpful services, as may the Consulate or Embassy of your home country. A must-read is *The Culture Map* [by Erin Meyer], a book exploring how to shift perspective to understand cultural differences and preferences, rather than learn from preventable mistakes.'

A gateway to Asia

Singapore's access to Asia does indeed make it uniquely placed for global business expansion. While Singapore is home to many cultures and languages, English is widely spoken in business pursuits – this is just one of many appealing factors about Singapore to foreign entrants to the market. It continues to function as a 'gateway' to Asia, and is appealing to global businesses for a number of reasons, including its vast market scale and size. Data from The Brookings Institution, for example, found that 55 per cent of the world's consumer class live in Asia.[10] Singapore's free trade agreements also grant ease of access to the nearby powerhouse economies of the Association of Southeast Asian Nations (ASEAN).

British-born expat Steve Settle has lived and worked in Singapore for more than 20 years. In 2013, he was tasked with bringing the CFO Centre to the country, which is a part-time financial director and CFO services provider. As the company's regional director, Steve oversees a locally based team consisting of Singaporeans and foreigners that assist founders and entrepreneurs to scale their businesses by implementing efficient financial functionality at the business support, operational and strategic levels. He says that while Singapore affords access to South-East Asia, expansion into each country should be approached with the same attention to localisation.

'People from other parts of the world don't appreciate the nuances of Asia, and there is often a perception that everything over here is part of China,' he noted. 'That's the challenge they have. They think the region is homogeneous; however, there are different languages, different cultures, different rules, different tax systems, different legal governance.

'If you want to access South-East Asia, you've got to be very clear on deciding where. If you have a product, you've got to do extensive research on which country is going to be the most receptive,' said Steve. 'There are businesses here that specialise in doing that kind of research, because you can make a huge mistake by going into the wrong place and burn a lot of money.'

> If you want to access South-East Asia, you've got to be very clear on deciding where. If you have a product, you've got to do extensive research on which country is going to be the most receptive.

Founder and managing partner of Chasm United, Amanda Goh has advised a diverse range of businesses on their corporate communications plans at a local and global level over the past 20 years. While Amanda is Singapore-based, like much of the city's population, her experience is highly international, having lived and worked in Malaysia, New York, Australia and London throughout her career. She started Chasm United to help founders, corporates and entrepreneurs navigate organisational transformation, risk management and communications.

Amanda notes that foreign businesses entering the Singapore market need to look at South-East Asia or ASEAN overall more holistically. 'Many overseas companies do underestimate the scale and access of Singapore to the rest of the region. If you look at Singapore only and not as a global jumping off point, you have missed an opportunity,' she said.

Navigating the cultural nuances of Singapore from a communications standpoint requires market sensing with trusted relationships and tact. 'Finding the middle ground, depending on your workforce and how they want to receive information, continues be really important in Singapore,' said Amanda. 'When all else fails, especially if you're trying to engage with a predominantly Singaporean talent pool, be direct, concise and have a very clear call to action.

'Because Singapore has a highly cosmopolitan culture, make sure that you're very clear on your targeting from your usual segments to like-minded individuals or "tribes". Businesses need to very clearly curate their communication with an Asia-first approach and to be very sensitive to both the local and foreign community groups.'

CHAPTER 15

JAPAN:
Mastery, shinrai and building relationships

Quick facts

Japan is referred to by its people as 'Nippon' or 'Nihon', which means 'Source of the Sun'. This is often translated into English as the 'Land of the Rising Sun'. General market information for Japan includes the following:

- Government: Unitary parliamentary constitutional monarchy
- Capital: Tokyo
- Population (at the time of writing): 125,340,995
- Official language: Japanese
- Currency: Japanese yen
- Area: 377,975 square kilometres (145,937 square miles)
- Nominal GDP for 2023: USD $4.234 trillion
- GDP per capita for 2023: USD $49,044
- GDP, purchasing power parity for 2023: USD $6.139 trillion

Japan's economy is market-oriented, highly developed, and now centred on the production of high-tech and precision goods. The following is a list of Japan's top industries:

- agriculture
- manufacturing

- fishing
- tourism.

Other important industries include mining, petroleum and rare earth metals exploration, and service industries.

Japan is also one of the leading economic and technological centres of the world. From the 1960s to the 1980s, it had one of the highest economic growth rates in the world. The objective that connects Japan's major policies with its future is the attainment of growth and development for its economy and society. The following are examples of how it is choosing to achieve this:

- high educational standards
- high investment rates in practical and useful equipment and tools
- positive labour-management relations
- easy access to cutting-edge technology and major investment in R&D
- a framework for global commerce that is more open
- a sizable domestic market with affluent customers, which has increased Japanese companies' ability to grow their operations.

Since 2011, foreign direct investment (FDI) in Japan has increased, and in 2020, the stock of FDI from outside reached a record high. These are some of the justifications for investing in Japan:

- increased commercial potential and creative possibilities
- good business conditions and internationally competitive regulations
- a place for entrepreneurs and innovators
- a stable political structure that supports the environment for business
- a labour force that is quite skilled, and renowned for being excellent employees committed to their businesses.

In 2016, Japanese SMEs made up 99.7 per cent of all enterprises and employed 32 million people, or roughly 68.8 per cent of the labour force in the private sector.

According to Japan's Immigration Services Agency, the number of foreign nationals residing in Japan as of the end of 2021 decreased by 4.4 per cent from the previous year to 2,760,635, marking the sharpest decline since the survey's inception in 1950. The majority of the immigrant population was Chinese (716,606), followed by Vietnamese (432,934) and South Koreans (409,855). All of the numbers were lower than they were the previous year.

For more information on the details included here, you can access the following resources:

- www.japan.go.jp
- www.imf.org
- www.worldometers.info
- www.asialinkbusiness.com.au
- www.jetro.go.jp/en/
- www.nippon.com/en/news.

***

Beyond the snow-clad mountains of Niseko, the fashionable shop fronts of Tokyo's Ginza, or the cherry blossom–lined temples in Kyoto, is a side to Japan that foreigners often overlook.

There is an abundance of business opportunity for international expansion – especially for those willing to invest time to understand its unique cultural, social and commercial nuances. This is a side to Japan that is certainly already well known to the 2.76 million foreigners living in the country – still a minority in comparison to the country's population of 125 million people. As the third largest economy in the world, Japan's economic size, scale and might is also undeniable.

Longevity and tradition is embedded in Japan's centuries-old cultural and commercial heritage. Of the world's 10 oldest companies still in operation, Japan is home to six, many of which have longstanding multi-generational ownership.[1] The oldest is Kongo Gumi, a construction company specialising in Buddhist temples, now headquartered in Osaka and established in 758 CE by a Korean immigrant.

Mastery

To this end, doing business in Japan requires mastery, driven by a commitment to – and respect for – continual learning. While establishing a business in Japan is one thing, it's quite another to maintain long-term success, like the centuries-old business of Kongo Gumi.

Time and patience are also needed in spades when taking business to the Japanese market from abroad. From feasibility research through to building local relationships, point of entry and beyond, it is a market that should be thoughtfully – and meticulously – approached when it comes to planning. This is in part due to Japan's relationship-focused, trust-based culture. But it's also a business culture of contrasts. Japan is innovative, quality-focused, entrepreneurial and forward moving. It's also built upon a highly structured society, steeped in tradition, rules and regulations when it comes to conducting business.

With the additional challenge of language barriers to navigate for those who do not natively speak Japanese, entering this market requires a measured approach and, as many of the business leaders discussed in this chapter demonstrate, a long-term commitment.

If mastery is about continuous learning, no shortcuts exist to successfully enter the Japanese market. Australian-born Melanie Brock AM, founder of her eponymous advisory firm based in Tokyo, has assisted a diverse range of businesses over the past 30 years in both the public and private sectors. Throughout her career, she has also led the charge in developing successful bilateral free trade agreements and architected regional Japan corporate social responsibility (CSR) activities. As one of Japan's most well regarded and respected APAC specialists, Melanie is a non-executive director on listed Japanese company boards, and also works with businesses looking to expand into – and outbound from – the Japanese market.

'In Japan, everything is more structured, and quite often formal. Some companies think they can skip that process and truncate it,' says Melanie. However, committing to the market and being patient does pay off, leading to longer lasting relationships.

In her experience, it's the interpersonal dynamics in the context of meetings that often trip people up. 'What I see very often is Australians are uncomfortable with a pause or silence. This is where patience and listening comes into practice. Drink the green tea, and listen,' she advises.

> ❝ What I see very often is Australians are uncomfortable with a pause or silence. This is where patience and listening comes into practice. Drink the green tea, and listen.

'I see the benefits of that beautifully developed trust that comes with listening, and the nuances, the kernels of information and the opportunities that are afforded to you, just because you were listening,' says Melanie.

In a society that is at once tied to its traditions, has powerful economic prowess and is eager to progress commercially, there is a balance to strike when looking to Japan to do business. Patience and perseverance are key, as is communication and building trust for long-term success.

Joshua Flannery, founder and CEO of Innovation Dojo, also notes the attention to the finest of communication details as part of building relationships in this market – which also supports the mission towards mastery. Innovation Dojo supports startup leaders through education and training, and leads a Global Mentorship Program and Kobe Startup Hub for Kobe City government.

'There are some other unofficial things to do with the team and the style of communicating. Can we work with this foreigner and the team? Do I understand the way they're speaking? Have they followed up? Have they sent the documents they said they were? Are they doing more than what we what we asked?' Joshua notes these are all questions any founder or business leader looking to do business in Japan should automatically consider, because even though business leaders in Japan are thinking this, they are rarely going to ask them.

A highly connected economy

The Japan of today is an open and welcoming economy. It's particularly amenable to foreign business, and its public and private sectors actively work to attract international investment and entrepreneurship. Many cities offer supportive launching pads for both startups and established businesses across many different sectors, from fine wine to coffee through to natural resources, infrastructure and technology.

However, even in our hyper-connected, globalised world, comparative to other major economies over the past two centuries, foreign business integration has been a slow and steady process – and Japan has not always been closely connected to the world and foreign business. An interesting point in its history came long before our digital age.

From 1603 and for the next 265 years, Japan's borders were almost entirely closed to foreigners. This period of prolonged commercial and cultural isolation was known as Sakoku, a policy that saw the Japanese economy turn inward. Sakoku was implemented at a government level as a measure to protect itself from religious and cultural influences from Europe and, during this time, Japan became an almost entirely self-sufficient economy. Locals were not permitted to leave, and very few foreigners, including trading partners, were allowed to enter. Japan eventually emerged, bringing with it an even more distinct cultural identity that was developed during this time, in which local and rural industries flourished, from sake-making to haiku poetry.[2]

It was the United States that effectively forced Japan to rejoin the world in 1853, when Commodore Matthew Calbraith Perry led his navy into Edo Bay, now Tokyo Bay. Since then, the United States' stake in the region has only grown – and it is now Japan's second largest trading partner following China.

In contrast to today, Japan's commercial and cultural connectedness to the world is highly integrated – with more opportunity still. Even during yet another (although not as long) form of isolation during the border closures of the COVID-19 pandemic, in the fiscal year of 2020, the government-affiliated Japan External Trade Organization (JETRO) assisted 1020 companies with market entry strategies. While only 96 of these established their bases in Japan or expanded into the market, this example highlights both the continued interest in the region, with the majority of parent companies coming from Asia (37.5 per cent), Europe (29.2 per cent) and North America (28.1 per cent).[3]

Even though Japan sits geographically within the Asia-Pacific region, it enjoys close trading ties, free trade agreements and economic partnerships with neighbouring economies and those from further afield. In 2015 the Japan–Australia Economic Partnership Agreement was established, making entry easier for Australian companies. Winemaker and wine distribution company Treasury Wine Estates took the opportunity in 2016 to expand its wine portfolio in the Japanese market, catering to the growing local demand for fine Australian and New Zealand wines.

Location matters

The first port of call for many international businesses in Japan is an obvious choice: the global business hub and burgeoning market of Tokyo. It sits within the Kanto region, home to the highest concentration of foreign-affiliated companies, with more than 70 per cent of head offices located there and almost 60 per cent in Tokyo, according to the latest JETRO statistics.

The nine regions in Japan are divided into 47 prefectures. While each region has its own cultural, social, industrial and geographic differences, they are unified, abiding by the same rule of law and regulations.

However, international businesses can benefit from understanding the different regions and prefectures, their populations, unique needs and business opportunities. The Kanagawa Prefecture, for example, also located within the Kanto region, is relatively small in population size, but is projected to be home to a highly aged population by 2050, when more than 30 per cent of its residents will be aged 70 or over.[4] This demographic has attracted business solutions to aid with the care of its elderly population, ranging from research endeavours to healthcare and more.

Another noteworthy prefecture with international opportunities is Fukuoka, which has frequently appeared in the top 25 cities in *Monocle* magazine's Quality of Life Survey – in good company with Tokyo and Kyoto. Fukuoka is also known as a gateway to East Asia, and has a strong automotive sector with manufacturing plants for the likes of Nissan, Toyota and Daihatsu located within the Kyushu region. In recent years, however, Fukuoka has also become an attractive base for startups locally and from overseas because of its lower cost of living comparative to the likes of Tokyo, liveability for young families and entrepreneurship accelerator and development programs. It has also been a focus of government initiatives to support new business, as well private sector investment, attracting billions of yen in venture capital funding in recent years.

Saitama City, which is located just 30 kilometres north of Tokyo, is also developing as a hub for business and innovation, with a particular focus on research and development equipment. As *The Japan Times* described, Saitama is 'in the vanguard of technological innovation'.[5]

Saitama and Fukuoka are just a couple of examples that signpost Japan's creative and commercial priorities at a government level over the coming years, with a national commitment to nurturing startups and entrepreneurship, and particularly those businesses that help to solve social issues.

Saitama is also the location of a new project that points to the city's success, with the influence of a foreign entity that has been successful in the Japanese market over the past three decades – Australian-originated construction and real estate group Lendlease.

The project – a data centre – broke ground in mid-2022 and is developed and constructed by Lendlease, via Lendlease Data Centre Partners (LLDCP) for Princeton Digital Group, a data services and internet infrastructure provider with global headquarters in Singapore.

A long-term approach

Lendlease entered the Japanese market in 1988, just before the 'Lost Decades', a period of economic stagnation caused by a collapse in asset prices from the early 1990s. Starting with a small team, Lendlease did not achieve instant success. But it was committed to the market and correctly spotted long-term potential for success.

From a sectoral perspective, expansion into Japan made perfect sense for a company such as Lendlease to scale and grow; Tokyo's real estate market is among the largest in the world. According to the Martin Prosperity Institute, and as reported in Bloomberg, 'Tokyo, the world's largest metro economy with USD $1.6 trillion in GDP-PPP, is just slightly smaller than all of South Korea. Were it a nation, Tokyo would rank as the 15th largest economy in the world.'[6]

In 1999, Andrew Gauci was Lendlease's 24th employee in Japan, and he has lived and worked in Japan for the business ever since, starting as project manager. Now Managing Director & CEO Japan, he said Lendlease's localisation strategy centred on a long-term commitment and hiring locally – but always working to bring something unique.

From the outset, the business hired locally, with only a small portion of the team – no more than four – employees being foreign, Andrew recalls.

'The majority of your workforce and your capability has to be local,' he says. 'You need to have all the right areas covered by locals, but have some international flavour. And those international people at the outset need to have a depth of understanding of the market.'

The turning point towards success for Lendlease in Japan was when the business shifted to third party project management, and with the development of a major office building in central Tokyo that introduced a new procurement system to the Japanese market.

While localising to operate within the commercial context of Japan is key to success, Andrew notes foreign entrants still need to bring something unique.

'You need a really good balance of understanding the market in Japan, and that obviously comes with time. But it's also about being able to bring in something different that's not in the market. Often people try to do too much of what they do elsewhere, or try and localise too much,' says Andrew. 'You need to localise sufficiently enough so that you can be accepted, but then bring in things that no-one else is doing.'

> You need a really good balance of understanding the market in Japan, and that obviously comes with time. But it's also about being able to bring in something different that's not in the market. Often people try to do too much of what they do elsewhere, or try and localise too much.

Lendlease's success has paved the way for more opportunities in the market, and the group has now delivered more than 1000 project management assignments and has a 500-strong local workforce.

Building trust

Nemawashi is a philosophy that is used in business team environments throughout Japan. In practice, nemawashi focuses on building consensus among team members and stakeholders. It's about understanding each stakeholder's position before a more formal meeting may take place. Although it's not a mandated business practice, foreign business leaders and their teams will encounter this way of working in Japan.

In Andrew's experience, however, some agility and flexibility is required. 'Yes, you do need nemawashi to some degree. But you won't be successful if all you are trying to do is please the nemawashi scenario.' He says that building long-term relationships is at the core of success in this market.

Former international rugby union player Ian Williams also knows the Japanese market in considerable depth, having first arrived in Japan in 1989. He played, to great success and acclaim, for both the Australia Wallabies and Japan Brave Blossoms, and his sporting career marked the starting point of what has become a three-decades-long career working between the two countries. In 2016, Ian was awarded the Japanese Foreign Minister's Commendation for service to the Japan–Australia relationship in business and sport. As a lawyer and non-executive director, Ian is a renowned strategic advisor to Japanese companies, and has also written extensively on the Japan–Australia trade and investment relationship throughout his career.

Ian has highlighted the differences in ways of working, which any foreign entrant to the market, particularly from Western cultures, should note. 'Your classic Australian business approach is "Hey, let's do some business together and build a relationship." Whereas in Japan and, it's "Let's build a relationship." And then there may be an opportunity to do business,' he says. 'The company that ended up being my biggest client as a law firm partner, I visited some 15 times before I had an opportunity to work with them. We're not very patient.'

The cultural norms of doing business in Japan are ultimately grounded in loyalty and trust. Pernille Rudlin is an expert on Japanese business and corporate culture, and has worked across both the United Kingdom and Japan throughout her career. She is fluent in spoken and written Japanese and lived locally in Japan for nine years. She worked for nearly a decade at Mitsubishi Corporation and was Director of External Relations, International Business at Fujitsu.

In her 2019 book, *Shinrai: Japanese Corporate Integrity in a Disintegrating Europe*, Rudlin examined one of the most important attributes of doing business in Japan – building trust. Shinrai is the Japanese word for 'trust', and Rudlin argues it's one of the most important attributes of doing business in Japan, and working with Japanese entities overseas. While her work has focused on building trust within multinational firms, her message is relevant to foreign enterprises of all sizes.

She writes:

Analysing the work I have done with clients over the past fifteen years, I would say there are five components of building trust in multinational companies. In sequential order they are communication, mutual interests, processes and regulations, reliability and accountability, and vision and values – and then back to communication again in a virtuous circle.

Rudlin argues trust can be nurtured when both parties (or multiple stakeholders) align on these key components.

Lessons in language

It seems quite deliberate that communication is listed by Rudlin first; language is one of the most difficult obstacles foreign businesses must overcome. Foreigners doing business in Japan say that speaking Japanese is highly advantageous when it comes to building all-important local relationships.

While English is spoken across the country, it's also worth noting that it was only in July 2017, in the lead-up to the Tokyo 2020 Olympics, that bilingual Japanese and English public signage was established in the Kanto capital.

'Having a common language is critical – this is why any initiative to help immigrants integrate into a society usually starts with language lessons,' writes Rudlin. 'The problem for Japan is that for native speakers of European languages, Japanese is one of the most difficult languages to learn, and Japanese feel similarly about English.'

> The problem for Japan is that for native speakers of European languages, Japanese is one of the most difficult languages to learn, and Japanese feel similarly about English.

The way forward, according to Rudlin, is a two-way effort. 'Japanese companies can do more to help Westerners learn Japanese – an intensive course in Japan is one of the most effective ways to do this,' she writes. 'Japanese companies can also communicate better than they do in English – it's not enough to make English the common language or force a minimum English level on employees, management needs to communicate vision, strategy and plans in English more effectively than it currently does.'

Part of the challenge of overcoming the language barrier comes back to mastery – which also brings us back to the need to respect Japan's unique culture and approach the market with a mindset focused on ongoing learning and understanding. While fluency in Japanese may not be a requirement, making an effort to reach some level of proficiency can pave the way for more meaningful business relationships in a market where trust, and the communication that can build on this trust, is so greatly valued.

CONCLUSION

THE JOURNEY CONTINUES

As I sit down to write this final element of *Decoding Global Growth*, I am filled with a sense of accomplishment and gratitude. The journey we've taken together through these pages has been a remarkable one, and I hope it has provided you with valuable insights, inspiration and guidance as you chart your course in the world of global expansion.

In the preceding chapters, we've explored the essential elements of global growth, from building a strong foundation to expanding your reach into foreign markets. We've delved into the intricacies of leadership, governance, storytelling and process management – the cornerstones upon which successful businesses are built. We have uncovered the secrets of scalability, and I have offered you the Process Scalability Formula as a tool to evaluate your readiness for growth. We have conducted a thorough examination of your business's potential through the Global Scalability Audit.

We have also discussed the critical aspects of your global journey, from identifying your target clients to creating a go-to-market strategy that resonates with your audience. We've emphasised the importance of building brand awareness in a foreign market and highlighted the significance of choosing the right distribution model, especially in light of the changes brought about by the COVID-19 pandemic.

But the journey doesn't end here. In fact, it's only just beginning. The road to global growth is an ongoing one, filled with challenges and opportunities at every turn. It requires adaptability, resilience and a commitment to continuous improvement.

As you move forward, I want to leave you with a few key take-aways that encapsulate the essence of our exploration:

- *Cultivate your network:* Your network is your greatest asset. Nurture it, expand it and use it to your advantage. The relationships you build will open doors and provide the support you need as you navigate the global landscape.

- *Embrace change:* The business world is constantly evolving, and successful global expansion requires adaptability. Stay open to new distribution models, emerging markets and innovative approaches to reaching your audience.

- *Invest in knowledge:* Knowledge is power. Continue to educate yourself about the markets you're entering, the industries you're operating in and the trends that shape them. Informed decisions are the bedrock of success.

- *Seek feedback:* Don't operate in isolation. Be coachable. Encourage feedback from your team, mentors and customers. Use their insights to refine your strategies and improve your processes.

- *Celebrate your successes:* Along the way, take a moment to celebrate your achievements, no matter how small they may seem. Acknowledge the progress you've made and the milestones you've reached. It's essential to stay motivated and inspired.

- *Pay it forward:* Just as I have shared my knowledge and experiences with you through this book, consider how you can pay it forward to others in your industry. Mentorship and collaboration are powerful tools for collective growth.

- *Stay curious:* The world is a vast and ever-changing place. Maintain your curiosity and hunger for learning. The more you explore, the more opportunities you'll discover.

Remember that this book is a guide, not a definitive roadmap. Your business is unique, and your journey will be too. While the principles and concepts presented here are universal, their application will depend on your specific circumstances and goals.

As I conclude this book, I want to express my sincere gratitude for joining me on this journey. Your ambition to expand your business's global reach is a testament to your entrepreneurial spirit and determination. I believe in your ability to succeed, and I am excited to witness the growth and impact you'll achieve.

The path ahead may be challenging, but it's also filled with untold possibilities. So, with a New York state of mind and a global perspective, set forth on your journey with confidence. You have the knowledge, the tools and the passion – now it's time to make your mark on the world.

May your business thrive on the global stage and continue to offer innovative solutions to the challenges of our time.

Thank you, and onwards to global success, however you define it.

IN THEIR OWN WORDS ...

During my interviews with the CEOs quoted through this book, I was curious to gain as much insight as possible. I asked all CEOs the following three questions:

1. What are your suggestions for 'recommended reading (or listening)' to other business leaders expanding globally?
2. What is your best piece of advice for companies that are expanding globally?
3. What are you most proud of?

I have provided here their answers in their own words.

Skander Malcolm, CEO OFX

www.ofx.com

Recommended reading or listening

Shoe Dog (Phil Knight) – captures the uncertainty (and opportunity) of going global well.

Best piece of advice for companies that are expanding globally

Accept that you will misjudge situations in ways you would not in your home market, but persevere with trusted partners because succeeding globally is very rewarding (and fun!).

What they are most proud of

Nurturing talent in lots of different parts of the world.

Neil Verdal-Austin, CEO SomnoMed

www.somnomed.com

Best piece of advice for companies that are expanding globally

Plan for extra time and bureaucratic delays. In this case, patience is a virtue for sure. It's still worth it but many of these issues are external and out of your control.

What they are most proud of

Promoting people within the organisation and allowing them to grow. Especially if they didn't see their own potential themselves – that's a joy to see.

Emma Lo Russo, Founder/CEO Digivizer

www.digivizer.com

Recommended reading or listening

- Reid Hoffman's *Masters of Scale* podcast series – one of the best to motivate you
- *10x is Easier than 2x* by Dan Sullivan
- *What Got You Here Won't Get You There* by Marshall Goldsmith
- *How Big Things Get Done* by Professor Bent Flyvbjerg & Dan Gardner
- *The Five Dysfunctions of a Team* by Patrick Lencioni
- *The Hard Things About Hard Things* by Ben Horowitz

Best piece of advice for companies that are expanding globally

Make expansion personal. You need to understand each country you are expanding to. That means spending time there, understanding the politics, social economics, industries and ecosystems. This helps grow your confidence about where to invest and about specific go-to-market nuances. Hiring the best people you can in each country can bring knowledge, relationships and networks that you couldn't otherwise do.

What they are most proud of

I am most proud of the fact that I am still happily married and have a beautiful and close relationship with my three children. Given the stress of building a global business and growing a family, I realise more and more over time how rare this is, to have worked so hard and been able to achieve both with a sense of fulfilment and joy (something I was determined to do).

Anthony Bastic, CEO AGB Events

www.agb.events

Recommended reading or listening

The *This Working Life* podcast, from Australian Broadcasting Corporation (ABC) Radio.

Best piece of advice for companies that are expanding globally

Formulating a successful global expansion strategy goes beyond just offering something entirely unique. It's also about delivering value with a nuanced touch that resonates with local audiences. This means adapting your products or services to align with cultural nuances while staying true to your brand identity and core values.

What they are most proud of

I take immense pride in the fact that our digital exhibition, 'Beauty Rich and Rare', became the first Australian exhibition to be curated into the prestigious Smithsonian Natural History Museum in Washington D.C. This milestone not only represents a significant global recognition but also underscores the educational and cultural impact of our work. It's a testament to our team's innovation and dedication, connecting audiences worldwide with Australia's diverse natural heritage. This accomplishment serves as a beacon of inspiration for our team and the wider community.

Phillip Campbell, CEO, enigmaFIT

www.enigmafit.com

Recommended reading or listening

Susan Lindner's LinkedIn top 20 podcast called *Innovation Storyteller* – she has a wonderful cross-section of guests and is humble, talented, funny, open and willing to help people on their life's journey. You can check it out at innovationstorytellers.com/podcasts.

Best piece of advice for companies that are expanding globally

Seize the moment with the five-minute meeting. We are all so busy, and our time is precious and limited. All too quickly, our judgment of a person or connection can be, 'No, too busy to catch up!'

I would always encourage you to be open to a five-minute catch-up, a quick introduction or a casual connection to a new colleague, because you never know where it might lead. A five-minute introduction of two American Chamber of Commerce members at a lunch networking event in 2016 resulted in a successful, ongoing partnership (and now a personal friendship) to launch in one of the most alluring, yet demanding, global cities – New York.

This was literally after a quick five-minute catch-up at the end of a function. Trena Blair was leaving for New York in four days. I was looking to launch our company in New York a few months later. So, after our five-minute catch-up, we decided on a coffee catch-up on the Sunday (two days before Trena was leaving for New York). Trena's grasp of engimaFIT's strategies, goals and launch concepts was very quick. We agreed that day over coffee that she would explore her extensive network of New York–based executives and guide engimaFIT's launch. Additionally, she sourced launch venues, introductions to banks and accountants, and advised on fundamentals of how to do business in New York. Her secret know-how knowledge and her impressive contact list were invaluable.

The result: with Trena's assistance and network, senior executives from major organisations attended our invitation-only launch event in New York, including major banks, Boston Consulting Group, Estee Lauder and BCD Travel – and we got three new pieces of business from the launch alone. Wow, what more can I say?! That's Trena!

What they are most proud of

Having worked with top-tier executives and entrepreneurs globally, I am always humbled by their feedback, including how our Fluid Thinking program has made a major change in both their business and personal life – whether it's doubling sales, a considerable improvement in profit, enhanced strategic and social leadership skills, gaining an hour back in each day, or achieving a much better work–life balance so they can spend more time with their family and friends. This is extremely satisfying for me.

However, my latest book, *Brain Habits: The Science of Subconscious Success*, has enabled me to share with everyone that their brain is more powerful than they might have first thought. Encouraging individuals to take up the challenge of upgrading their brain for personal and professional success has been a long-term dream and goal come true.

ACKNOWLEDGEMENTS

For a first-time author, writing and publishing a book is daunting. Many colleagues have supported, guided and encouraged me as I have drafted, restructured and redrafted content. The finished product has taken a global village.

First, I am grateful to the clients who have trusted me for the last decade, allowing me to spearhead and oversee their USA expansion endeavours.

To the CEOs and founders I interviewed for the book: Anthony Bastic, Skander Malcolm, Emma Lo Russo, April White, Neil Verdal-Austin, Ben Ient and Phillip Campbell as well as subject matter experts Megan Todd and Justine Harvey. I am deeply grateful you entrusted me to tell your business success stories. I am inspired by your professionalism and leadership capabilities and honoured to have spent time with you while researching my book. Your patience as I've sought additional information, and especially your ongoing encouragement to 'keep at it', has been a critical factor in completing the book.

Many colleagues have also supported my book-writing endeavour.

First and foremost, I want to thank Jennifer Byrne, Andrew Chick and Jodie Baker, who have been on this journey with me from the beginning. I am incredibly grateful for your invaluable support and insightful reviews of my book; your encouragement and generosity has been truly uplifting.

Kate McCallum and Jane Turner educated me on the process of writing and publishing a book. Their gentle, honest assessment of the journey I was to embark on assisted my understanding of the project's rewarding but sometimes overwhelming nature. I'm grateful for their generosity in sharing their considerable experience both as authors and supporting writers, including the traps to avoid and tips to succeed.

My book was completed because of the extraordinary support from Kate Racovolis. Our collaboration is one I cherish and will always recollect fondly. Kate gave me the confidence to continue during the most challenging times. Kate's incredible gift as a writer and journalist shines in chapters 11 to 15, as she led the interviewing and writing of these essential market insights.

I'm deeply grateful to my wonderful colleagues Esmarie Talidasan, Amanda Leigh Doueihi, Margot Andersen, Kerryn Colen and Susan Campbell, who provided valuable feedback at various stages.

To my self-publishing team – Michael Hanrahan, Charlotte Duff (editor extraordinaire) and Anna Clemann – thank you for putting the final steps in place to make this book a reality.

To the contributors in the five markets – Australia, the United States, the United Kingdom, Singapore and Japan – I'm deeply grateful for your generosity of time to share your insights and the opportunity to illuminate your impressive work.

Thank you to the following:

- Australia: David Chilver, Melissa Keir, Gennaro Autore, Charlene Batson.

- United States: Gemma Lloyd, Lee-Martin Seymour, Almira Armstrong, Jennifer Byrne.

- United Kingdom: Nicky Valentine, Bobby Lane, Demetrio Zema, Justin Webb.

- Singapore: Elly Both, Steve Settle, Amanda Goh.

- Japan: Melanie Brock, Joshua Flannery, Andrew Gauci, Ian Williams, Pernille Rudlin.

To my cherished husband, Christian, for your steadfast encouragement to 'embrace courage', which continues to echo within me as I release my first book into the world. Your boundless patience, constant motivation and enduring love have been the driving force behind my ability to pen these words onto these pages.

ABOUT THE AUTHOR

Trena Blair is an international multi-award-winning businesswoman, company director and CEO of FD Global Connections – a concierge advisory firm specialising in scaleup and growth strategies.

Throughout her 20-year career, she has effortlessly spanned corporate and entrepreneurial communities, working with organisations to deliver highly specialised international expansion strategies to access the US market.

Trena has been named by Forbes as an 'expert in expanding business from Australia into the US'. In recognition of her services to the business community globally and as a leader, in 2023, Trena was the recipient of the Gold Stevie® Award for Best Female Entrepreneur (Business Services) and, in 2022, for Best Female Entrepreneur Asia, Australia or New Zealand.

A regular media commentator, Trena has been featured on major outlets, including *The Financial Review* and *Sky Business News*, and is a keynote speaker in Sydney, New York and London. This is her first book.

ENDNOTES

Chapter 1 – Blending the past with the present

1   Rob Koopman, Wikimedia Commons, licensed under the Creative Commons Attribution-Share Alike 2.0 Generic license.
2   Kolb, M (2018, updated 2021), 'What is globalization? And how has the global economy shaped the United States?', Peterson Institute for International Economics.
3   World Trade Organization (2013), 'Trends in international trade', *World Trade Report 2013: Factors shading the future of world trade,* World Trade Organization.
4   www.statista.com/statistics/264682/worldwide-export-volume-in-the-trade-since-1950
5   See, for example, Groth, G, Esposito, M & Tse, T (2023), *The Great Remobilization: Strategy and Design for a Smarter Global Future*, Random House US.
6   Brooks, D (2022), 'Globalization is over. The global culture wars have begun', *The New York Times*, 8 April.
7   White, O, Woetzel, J, Smit, S, Seong, J & Devesa, T (2023), 'The complication of concentration in global trade', McKinsey Global Institute, 12 January.
8   Logan, A (2019), 'What is a scaleup?', Tech Nation.

Chapter 2 – Pioneering entrepreneurs from the past

1   HistoryWorld (2012), 'Time: Venice, Years 259–1958', Oxford Reference, www.oxfordreference.com/display/10.1093/acref/9780191736599.timeline.0001.
2   (2021), 'History of banks – part 2', Secure Cash, www.securecash.com.au/blog/history-of-banks-part-2/.
3   Photograph © Trena Blair.
4   CFI Team (2020), 'Double entry', Corporate Finance Institute, www.corporatefinanceinstitute.com/resources/accounting/double-entry.
5   For more on this topic, also see Kelly, N (2015), '7 traits of companies on the fast track to international growth', *Harvard Business Review*, 6 March.
6   Anderson, S, Platzer, M (2006), *American Made: The Impact of Immigrant Entrepreneurs and Professionals on US Competitiveness*, National Venture Capital Association.
7   ibid.
8   Hathaway, I (2017), 'Almost half of Fortune 500 companies were founded by American immigrants or their children', The Brookings Institution.
9   CGU (2018), *Migrant Small Business Report: Celebrating the Migrant Small Business Owners Building Australia*, CGU.

10 Gallop (2018), *Three Requirements of a Diverse and Inclusive Culture – and Why They Matter for Your Organization*, Gallop, Inc.
11 Enterprise IT (2005), 'From hobby to foreign exchange service', *The Age*, 14 October.
12 OFX (2021), *Annual Report*, OFX Group Limited.

Chapter 3 – Considering the journey ahead
1 Kepka, A (2020, updated 2022), 'Business startup statistics Australia', fundsquire.
2 Entrepreneur staff (2023), 'Unique selling proposition (USP)', *Small Business Encyclopedia*, Entrepreneur.
3 You can read more about this tool at Thomson's website: www.peterjthomson.com/2013/11/value-proposition-canvas/.
4 Barnatt-Smith, R (2023), '6 reasons why your startup is suffering from high employee turnover', Startup Nation, 5 April.
5 Startup Genome (2023), Global Startup Ecosystem Report 2023, https://startupgenome.com/reports/scaleup-report.
6 Baker, M (2020), 'How to reduce the risk of employee change fatigue', Gartner.
7 Figure sourced from Kristóf, P (2016), 'How established companies can master disruptive innovation like startups? Achieving innovation excellence and disruptive ability', PhD dissertation.
8 Data sourced from Hillenbrand, P, Kiewell, D, Miller-Cheevers, R, Ostojic, I & Springer, G (2019), *Traditional company, new businesses: The pairing that can ensure an incumbent's survival*, McKinsey & Company.

Chapter 4 – The leadership characteristics of a global entrepreneur
1 IMD (2023), 'World Competitiveness Ranking', International Institute for Management Development, https://www.imd.org/centers/wcc/world-competitiveness-center/rankings/world-competitiveness-ranking/
2 (2023), 'Business abroad: How an Aussie company expanded overseas', *Corporate Traveller*.
3 www.abs.gov.au/statistics/economy/international-trade/international-trade-supplementary-information-financial-year/latest-release
4 Azoulay, P, Jones, BF, Kim, DJ & Miranda, J (2018), 'Research: The average age of a successful startup founder is 45', *Harvard Business Review*, 11 July.
5 ibid.
6 Maritz, A (2021), 'Contrary to popular belief, middle-aged entrepreneurs do better', *The Conversation*, 28 April.

Chapter 5 – Governance structures as your business grows
1 Allen TD, Eby LT, Poteet ML, Lentz E & Lima L (2004), 'Career benefits associated with mentoring for protégé: a meta-analysis', *J Appl Psychol*, Feb;89(1):127–36.

2   Broekman, L (2021), *State of the Market Global Report 2021*, Global Research Council; Advisory Board Centre; Research lead: Louise Broekman.

3   (2023), 'What is governance?', Governance Institute of Australia, www.governanceinstitute.com.au/resources/what-is-governance/.

Chapter 6 – Storytelling techniques to secure funding

1   Fryer, B (2003), 'Storytelling that moves people', *Harvard Business Review*.

2   (2016), 'Stories stick and there is the science to prove it', FIPP.com, www.fipp.com/news/stories-stick-and-there-is-the-science-to-prove-it/#.

3   Copie de gravure ancienne, unknown author, Wikimedia Commons, image in the public domain.

Chapter 7 – The Scalability Formula for success

1   Zook, C & Allen, J (2012), *Repeatability: Build Enduring Businesses for a World of Constant Change*, Harvard Business Review Press.

2   Tighe, D (2022), 'Revenue share of Nike worldwide in the fiscal year of 2022, by product category', Statista.

3   Gorelik, I (2021), 'How brands can deliver a support experience customers will rave about', *Forbes*, 29 July.

4   Nolden, C (2021), 'The importance of personalized customer service in 2021', Burrelles, 24 August.

5   Stone, A (2012), 'Why waiting is torture', *The New York Times*, 18 August.

6   Brown, V (2015), 'Australian's spend more than 58,000 days in a line at the Post Office, according to study', news.com.au.

7   Tšernov, K (nd), 'The cost of queues: How improper queue management affects your bottom line', Qminder.com.

8   Bump, P (2020), 'Predictive marketing: What it is & how to leverage it', hubspot.com.

9   Brecht, J (2021), 'How to use probability theory for smarter social media marketing', LinkedIn, 20 June.

10   Richards-Gustafson, F (nd), 'Approaches to organizational strategic alignment', Chron.com.

11   APM (2021), 'What is configuration management?', *APM Body of Knowledge*, 7th ed, Association for Project Management.

12   Amadea, Ron (2020), 'Andy Rubin's smartphone startup, Essential, is dead', arstechnica.com.

13   Gurman, M & Barinka, A (2018), 'Android creator puts Essential up for sale, cancels next phone', Bloomberg, 25 May.

14   Pipedrive (nd), 'Lessons on scaling your business globally (and quickly)', www.pipedrive.com/en/blog/scaling-business-globally.

Chapter 8 – The customer quest: Developing your go-to-market strategy

1   Mohammed, S (2020), 'Business strategy lessons from [yellow tail]: Case study & blue ocean strategy', Medium.com, shahmm.medium.com/business-strategy-lessons-from-yellowtail-blue-ocean-strategy-e139ce6f7ca2.

2   ibid.

3   Arturo Conde (2023, updated), 'The House passes the $1.85 trillion Build Back Better Act. Here's what's in it', 22 August, https://smartasset.com/financial-advisor/biden-infrastructure-plan.

4   Blank, S (2010), 'Perfection by subtraction – the minimum feature set', steveblank.com/2010/03/04/perfection-by-subtraction-the-minimum-feature-set/.

5   CB Research (2021), 'The top 12 reasons startups fail', CB Information Services.

6   McLachlan, S (2021), 'How to create a buyer persona', Hootsuite, blog.hootsuite.com/buyer-persona/.

7   Quoted in Andrivet, M (2022), 'A simple definition of brand positioning', *The Branding Journal*, 9 March.

Chapter 9 – Sales and distribution strategies

1   Zoltners, A, Sinha, P & Lorimer, S (2019), 'Technology is blurring the line between field sales and inside sales', *Harvard Business Review*, 1 October.

Chapter 10 – Building a global brand

1   Guerrieria, M (2023), 'Revealed: The world's most valuable brands of 2023', Kantar, 14 June.

2   Hamill, A (2020), 'Les Binet on why long-term marketing matters in the age of short-termism', WARC, www.warc.com/newsandopinion/opinion/les-binet-on-why-long-term-marketing-matters-in-the-age-of-short-termism/en-gb/3307.

3   Faria, J (2023), 'Leading advertisers worldwide in 2021, by ad spending', Statista.

4   Forsey, C (2022), 'Marketing budget: How much should your team spend in 2023? [By industry]', HubSpot, https://blog.hubspot.com/marketing/marketing-budget-percentage.

5   Beach, H (2022), 'The hilarious translation mistake KFC China made with its slogan', Mashed, 26 January.

Chapter 11 – Australia: Fighting the tyranny of distance

1   Economist Intelligence Unit (2023), *The Global Liveability Index 2023*, The Economist Intelligence Unit Ltd.

2   ABS (2022), 'Australia's population by country of birth', Australian Bureau of Statistics, 26 April.

3   For more information, see www.reconciliation.org.au/reconciliation/acknowledgement-of-country-and-welcome-to-country.

4   For more information, see www.dfat.gov.au/trade/agreements/trade-agreements.

5 See www.austrade.gov.au/international/invest/importance-of-foreign-direct-investment/economic-activity-of-foreign-owned-businesses-in-australia to explore the data from this report.

6 (2012), 'Dropbox drops into Dublin', Datacentre.me, datacentre.me/blog/dropbox-drops-into-dublin/.

7 Terlato, P (2016), 'Australians are global leaders in contactless card payments', finder.com.au.

8 Cave, D (2017, updated 2018), 'The New York Times in Australia? Yes. Here's why', *The New York Times*, 20 September.

9 ABS (2022), 'Counts of Australian businesses, including entries and exits', Australian Bureau of Statistics, 25 August.

10 (2022), 'SMEs are the lifeblood of the Australian Economy', Australian Banking Association.

Chapter 12 – The United States: The complexity trap

1 Damgaard, J & Sánchez-Muñoz, C (2022), 'United States is world's top destination for foreign direct investment', IMFBlog, International Monetary Fund.

2 BEA (2022), 'New foreign direct investment in the United States, 2021', Bureau of Economic Analysis, 6 July.

3 Hathaway, I (2017), 'Almost half of Fortune 500 companies were founded by American immigrants or their children', The Brookings Institution.

4 Perry, MJ (2019), 'US State GDPs compared to entire countries', FEE Stories, Foundation for Economic Education.

5 CNBC.com staff (2022), 'America's top states for business 2022: The full rankings', CNBC.com, 13 July.

6 For more information, see www.researchtriangle.org/the-triangle/.

7 For more information, see corplaw.delaware.gov/delawares-benefits-international-business/.

8 Glasner, J (2021), 'These countries have the most startup investment for their size', crunchbase news.

Chapter 13 – The United Kingdom: Breaking through in a crowded market

1 Lokun, J (2022), '4 leadership lessons we can learn from Queen Elizabeth II', *Entrepreneur*, 13 September.

2 Schott, B (2022), 'Brand Britannia and the Marmite monarchy', Bloomberg.com, 16 September.

3 See, for example, Frick, J, Edwards, D, Adam, E & Cazacu, A (2021), 'US companies show strong confidence in the UK as a place to do business', Bain & Company, 12 July.

4   Luttig, V (2022), 'The UK remains Europe's most attractive destination for financial services investment, but the gap with France narrows further', press release, Ernst & Young, 13 June.

5   England, J (2021), 'UK ranked second to US for fintech capital funding in 2020', *FinTech*, 21 January.

6   Statista Research Department (2023), 'Advertising in the United Kingdom (UK) – statistics & facts', Statista.

7   (2023), *Public Relations & Communication Activities in the UK – Market Size 2011–2029*, IBISWorld.

Chapter 14 – Singapore: Navigating cultural heritage

1   Statista Research Department (2023), 'Population in Singapore in 2022, by citizenship status', Statista, 22 May.

2   (2021), 'Dyson looks to Singapore for new talent', *HR Asia*, 16 April.

3   Statista Research Department (2023), 'Number of unicorn startups in Singapore in 2021, by industry', Statista, 22 May.

4   Statista Research Department (2023), 'Number of unicorn startups with cross-border investments in Singapore in 2021, by activity', Statista, 22 May.

5   Vaswani, K (2021), 'Grab: How an Uber killer became a powerful Asian super-app', BBC News, 3 May.

6   (2018), 'Grab goes hyper-local in its expansion strategy', WARC, 15 November.

7   Shu, C (2021), 'Australia-based Employment Hero raises $45M AUD for its global expansion', TechCrunch, 2 March.

8   To listen to the full talk, go to mediacast.smu.edu.sg/media/REMAINING+OURSELVES+IN+THE+GLOBAL+CITY/1_7m1kcne7/130830192.

9   For more information on this, go to www.greenplan.gov.sg.

10 Buchholz, K (2021), 'Asia's consumer class is growing. This chart shows how', World Economic Forum.

Chapter 15 – Japan: Mastery, shinrai and building relationships

1   Pariona, A (2017), 'The oldest companies still operating today', World Atlas.

2   Oe, H (2022), 'How centuries of self-isolation turned Japan into one of the most sustainable societies on Earth', *The Conversation*, 10 August.

3   JETRO (2021), *Invest Japan Report 2021*, Japan External Trade Organization.

4   Takeuchi, M & Tomomatsu, I (2018), 'Prevention, intervention, and control of an individual's state of health – ME-BYO concept in Kanagawa Prefecture', *J Community Med Health Educ*, Vol 8.

5   (2018), 'Saitama in the vanguard of technological innovation', *The Japan Times*, 23 January.

6   Florida, R (2017), 'The economic power of cities compared to nations', Bloomberg.com, 17 March.